grandma's best
100 everyday recipes

First published in 2013
LOVE FOOD is an imprint of Parragon Books Ltd

Parragon
Chartist House
15-17 Trim Street
Bath BA1 1HA, UK

www.parragon.com/lovefood

ISBN: 978-1-4723-1265-5

Printed in China.

Notes for the Reader

This book uses both metric and imperial measurements. Follow the same units of measurement throughout;
do not mix metric and imperial. All spoon measurements are level: teaspoons are assumed to be 5 ml, and
tablespoons are assumed to be 15 ml. Unless otherwise stated, milk is assumed to be full fat, eggs and individual vegetables are medium, and pepper is freshly ground black pepper. Unless otherwise stated, all root
vegetables should be washed in plain water and peeled prior to using. Garnishes, decorations and serving
suggestions are all optional and not necessarily included in the recipe ingredients or method.

The times given are an approximate guide only. Preparation times differ according to the techniques used by
different people and the cooking times may also vary from those given. Optional ingredients, variations or
serving suggestions have not been included in the time calculations.

Recipes using raw or very lightly cooked eggs should be avoided by infants, the elderly, pregnant women,
convalescents and anyone suffering from an illness. Pregnant and breastfeeding women are advised to avoid
eating peanuts and peanut products. Sufferers from nut allergies should be aware that some of the ready-
made ingredients used in the recipes in this book may contain nuts. Always check the packaging before
use.

grandma's
best

introduction

The kitchen is the heart of the home and, for many, Grandma is the heart of the kitchen. It was Grandma who created wonderful culinary memories for us and we yearn for those delicious foods that evoke happy remembrances of home cooking. You'll find all those recipes — and those memories — in this collection.

There's a range of simple but satisfying dishes from warming soups to quick pasta dishes that deliver instant comfort. Why not try Mushrooms on Toast or Corned Beef Hash for a leisurely brunch? Or Fried Chicken Wings or Steak Sandwiches for a quick snack after a busy day?

All the recipes you need to create the perfect weekend lunch are here, from roasts and pies to satisfying stews and casseroles. To accompany these are the essential side dishes - perfect roast potatoes, home-made gravy and delicious vegetables. These are sure to impress family and friends and will create warm memories for the next generation.

For dessert, you are spoilt for choice with a whole chapter of delicious dishes – from winter warmers like Bread and Butter Pudding and Pumpkin Pie to summer treats such as Banana Splits.

The irresistible smell of warm baking is the essence of Grandma's home cooking, and this section offers the whole range from simple cookies and muffins to special celebration cakes. There's also a couple of straightforward bread recipes which will fill the house with tempting aromas. These may just disappear before they have had time to cool!

Whether you consider yourself an experienced cook or are just starting out, we're sure that this collection will soon become a well-used treasure. In *Grandma's Best – 100 Everyday Recipes*, you'll find a diverse and delicious range of recipes, and each one comes with clear step-by-step instructions and photos to guarantee results just as good as Grandma's!

simple but satisfying

tomato soup

ingredients

serves 4

55 g/2 oz butter
1 onion, finely chopped
700 g/1 lb 9 oz tomatoes,
    finely chopped
600 ml/1 pint hot chicken stock
    or vegetable stock
pinch of sugar
2 tbsp shredded fresh
    basil leaves, plus extra
    sprigs, to garnish
1 tbsp chopped fresh parsley
salt and pepper
chilli oil, for drizzling (optional)

method

1 Melt half the butter in a large, heavy-based saucepan.
   Add the onion and cook over a low heat, stirring
   occasionally, for 5 minutes, or until softened. Add the
   tomatoes, season to taste with salt and pepper and
   cook for 5 minutes.

2 Pour in the hot stock, bring back to the boil, then
   reduce the heat and cook for 10 minutes.

3 Push the soup through a sieve with the back of a
   wooden spoon to remove the tomato skins and seeds.
   Return to the saucepan and stir in the sugar, remaining
   butter, basil and parsley. Heat through briefly, but do
   not allow to boil.

4 Ladle into warmed soup bowls. Serve immediately,
   garnished with a sprig of basil and a drizzle of chilli oil,
   if using.

split pea & ham soup

ingredients

serves 6–8

500 g/1 lb 2 oz split green peas
1 tbsp olive oil
1 large onion, finely chopped
1 large carrot, finely chopped
1 celery stick, finely chopped
1 litre/1¾ pints chicken stock or
    vegetable stock
1 litre/1¾ pints water
225 g/8 oz lean smoked ham,
    finely diced
¼ tsp dried thyme
¼ tsp dried marjoram
1 bay leaf
salt and pepper

method

1 Rinse the peas under cold running water. Put them in a saucepan and cover generously with water. Bring to the boil and boil for 3 minutes, skimming off the foam from the surface. Drain the peas.

2 Heat the oil in a large saucepan over a medium heat. Add the onion and cook for 3–4 minutes, stirring occasionally, until just softened. Add the carrot and celery and continue cooking for 2 minutes.

3 Add the peas, pour over the stock and water and stir to combine.

4 Bring just to the boil and stir the ham into the soup. Add the thyme, marjoram and bay leaf. Reduce the heat, cover and cook gently for 1–1½ hours, until the ingredients are very soft. Remove the bay leaf.

5 Taste and adjust the seasoning. Ladle into warmed soup bowls and serve.

chicken noodle soup

ingredients

serves 4–6

2 skinless chicken breasts
1.2 litres/2 pints water or chicken
    stock
3 carrots, sliced into 5-mm/¼-inch
    slices
85 g/3 oz egg noodles
salt and pepper
fresh tarragon leaves, to garnish

method

1 Place the chicken breasts in a large saucepan over a medium heat, add the water and bring to a simmer. Cook for 25–30 minutes. Skim any foam from the surface if necessary. Remove the chicken from the stock and keep warm.

2 Continue to simmer the stock, add the carrots and noodles and cook for 4–5 minutes.

3 Thinly slice or shred the chicken breasts and place in warmed serving bowls.

4 Season the soup to taste with salt and pepper and pour over the chicken. Serve immediately, garnished with the tarragon.

steak sandwiches

ingredients

makes 4 sandwiches

8 thick slices white or brown bread
butter, for spreading
2 handfuls mixed salad leaves
3 tbsp olive oil
2 onions, thinly sliced
675 g/1 lb 8 oz rump or sirloin
    steak, about 2.5 cm/1 inch
    thick
1 tbsp Worcestershire sauce
2 tbsp wholegrain mustard
2 tbsp water
salt and pepper

method

1 Spread each slice of bread with some butter and add a few salad leaves to the bottom slices.

2 Heat 2 tablespoons of the oil in a large, heavy-based frying pan over a medium heat. Add the onions and cook, stirring occasionally, for 10–15 minutes until softened and golden brown. Using a slotted spoon, transfer to a plate and set aside.

3 Increase the heat to high and add the remaining oil to the pan. Add the steak, season to taste with pepper and cook quickly on both sides to seal. Reduce the heat to medium and cook, turning once, for 2½–3 minutes each side for rare or 3½–5 minutes each side for medium. Transfer the steak to a plate.

4 Add the Worcestershire sauce, mustard and water to the pan and stir to deglaze by scraping any sediment from the base of the pan. Return the onions to the pan, season to taste with salt and pepper and mix well.

5 Thinly slice the steak across the grain, divide between the four bottom slices of bread and cover with the onions. Cover with the top slices of bread and press down gently. Serve immediately.

ham & cheese sandwich

ingredients

makes 1 sandwich

2 slices country-style bread,
  such as white Italian bread,
  thinly sliced
20 g/¾ oz butter, at room
  temperature
55 g/2 oz Gruyère cheese, grated
1 slice cooked ham, trimmed to fit
  the bread, if necessary

method

1 Thinly spread each slice of bread on one side with
  butter, then put one slice on the work surface, buttered
  side down. Sprinkle half the cheese over, taking it to the
  edge of the bread, then add the ham and top with the
  remaining cheese. Add the other slice of bread,
  buttered side up, and press down.

2 Heat a heavy-based frying pan, ideally non-stick,
  over a medium–high heat until hot. Reduce the heat
  to medium, add the sandwich and fry on one side for
  2–3 minutes, until golden brown.

3 Flip the sandwich over and fry on the other side for
  2–3 minutes, until all the cheese is melted and the
  bread is golden brown. Cut the sandwich in half
  diagonally and serve immediately.

tuna melts

ingredients
makes 4 melts

4 slices sourdough bread
400 g/14 oz canned tuna,
    drained and flaked
4 tbsp mayonnaise, or to taste
1 tbsp Dijon mustard or
    wholegrain mustard,
    plus extra, to taste
4 spring onions, chopped
2 tbsp dill pickle or sweet pickle,
    to taste
1 hard-boiled egg, shelled and
    finely chopped
1 small carrot, grated
1 tbsp capers in brine, rinsed and
    roughly chopped
2 tbsp chopped fresh parsley or
    chives
handful of lettuce leaves
8 thin slices red Cheddar cheese
salt and pepper

method

1 Preheat the grill to high and position the grill rack
    about 10 cm/4 inches from the heat source. Line a
    baking sheet with foil and set aside. Place the bread
    on the grill rack and toast for 2 minutes on each side,
    or until crisp and lightly browned.

2 Meanwhile, put the tuna in a bowl with the
    mayonnaise and mustard and beat together to
    break up the tuna. Add the spring onions, pickle,
    egg, carrot, capers, and salt and pepper to taste
    and beat together, adding extra mayonnaise or
    mustard to taste. Stir in the parsley.

3 Put the toast on the foil-lined baking sheet and top
    each slice with a lettuce leaf. Divide the tuna salad
    between the slices of toast and spread out. Top each
    melt with cheese slices, cut to fit.

4 Place under the grill and grill for 2 minutes, or until
    the cheese is melted and very lightly browned. Transfer
    to a plate and serve immediately.

pasta with pesto

ingredients

serves 4

450 g/1 lb dried tagliatelle
salt
fresh basil leaves, to garnish

pesto

2 garlic cloves
25 g/1 oz pine kernels
115 g/4 oz fresh basil leaves
55 g/2 oz freshly grated Parmesan
    cheese
125 ml/4 fl oz olive oil
salt

method

1 To make the pesto, put the garlic, pine kernels, a large pinch of salt and the basil into a mortar and pound to a paste with a pestle. Transfer to a bowl and gradually work in the cheese with a wooden spoon, then add the olive oil to make a thick, creamy sauce. Taste and adjust the seasoning, if necessary.

2 Alternatively, put the garlic, pine kernels and a large pinch of salt into a blender or food processor and process briefly. Add the basil and process to a paste. With the motor still running, gradually add the olive oil. Scrape into a bowl and beat in the cheese. Taste and adjust the seasoning, if necessary.

3 Bring a large saucepan of lightly salted water to the boil. Add the pasta, bring back to the boil and cook for 8–10 minutes, or until tender but still firm to the bite.

4 Drain well, return to the saucepan and toss with half the pesto, then divide between warmed serving plates and top with the remaining pesto. Garnish with the basil leaves and serve.

macaroni cheese

ingredients

serves 4

250 g/9 oz dried macaroni
55 g/2 oz butter, plus extra for
  cooking the pasta
600 ml/1 pint milk
⅛ tsp grated nutmeg
55 g/2 oz plain flour
200 g/7 oz mature Cheddar
  cheese, grated
55 g/2 oz Parmesan cheese, grated
200 g/7 oz baby spinach
salt and pepper

method

1 Cook the macaroni according to the instructions on the packet. Remove from the heat, drain, add a small knob of butter to keep it soft, return to the saucepan and cover to keep warm.

2 Put the milk and nutmeg into a saucepan over a low heat and heat until warm, but don't boil. Put the butter into a heavy-based saucepan over a low heat. Melt the butter, add the flour and stir to make a roux. Cook gently for 2 minutes. Add the milk a little at a time, whisking it into the roux, then cook for about 10–15 minutes to make a smooth sauce.

3 Add three quarters of the Cheddar cheese and Parmesan cheese and stir through until they have melted in. Add the spinach, season to taste with salt and pepper and remove from the heat.

4 Preheat the grill to high. Put the macaroni into a shallow heatproof dish, then pour the sauce over. Scatter the remaining cheese over the top and place the dish under the preheated grill. Grill until the cheese begins to brown, then serve immediately.

spaghetti bolognese

ingredients

serves 4

1 tbsp olive oil
1 onion, finely chopped
2 garlic cloves, chopped
1 carrot, chopped
1 celery stick, chopped
50 g/1¼ oz pancetta or streaky
    bacon, diced
350 g/12 oz fresh lean beef mince
400 g/14 oz canned chopped
    tomatoes
2 tsp dried oregano
125 ml/4 fl oz red wine
2 tbsp tomato purée
350 g/12 oz dried spaghetti
salt and pepper
chopped fresh parsley, to garnish

method

1 Heat the oil in a large frying pan. Add the onion and cook for 3 minutes. Add the garlic, carrot, celery and pancetta and sauté for 3–4 minutes, or until just beginning to brown.

2 Add the beef and cook over a high heat for another 3 minutes or until all of the meat is browned. Stir in the tomatoes, oregano and wine and bring to the boil. Reduce the heat, cover and leave to simmer for about 45 minutes.

3 Stir in the tomato purée and season to taste with salt and pepper.

4 Bring a large saucepan of lightly salted water to the boil. Add the pasta, bring back to the boil and cook for 8–10 minutes, until tender but still firm to the bite. Drain thoroughly.

5 Transfer the spaghetti to serving plates and pour over the bolognese sauce. Toss to mix well, garnish with parsley and serve hot.

mushrooms on toast

ingredients

serves 4

12 slices baguette, each 1 cm/
½ inch thick, or 2 individual
baguettes, cut lengthways
3 tbsp olive oil
2 garlic cloves, crushed
225 g/8 oz chestnut mushrooms,
sliced
225 g/8 oz mixed wild mushrooms
2 tsp lemon juice
2 tbsp chopped fresh parsley
salt and pepper

method

1 Preheat the grill to medium–high. Place the slices of baguette on a ridged griddle pan and toast on both sides until golden. Reserve and keep warm.

2 Meanwhile, heat the oil in a frying pan. Add the garlic and cook gently for a few seconds, then add the chestnut mushrooms. Cook, stirring constantly, over a high heat for 3 minutes. Add the wild mushrooms and cook for a further 2 minutes. Stir in the lemon juice.

3 Season to taste with salt and pepper and stir in the chopped parsley.

4 Spoon the mushroom mixture onto the warm toast and serve immediately.

simple savoury beef

ingredients

serves 4

55 g/2 oz butter
1 onion, finely chopped
2 carrots, finely chopped
4 tomatoes, peeled and chopped
25 g/1 oz plain flour
1 tsp mustard powder
600 ml/1 pint beef stock
500 g/1 lb 2 oz fresh beef mince
175 g/6 oz frozen peas
salt and pepper
chopped fresh parsley, to garnish

method

1 Melt the butter in a saucepan. Add the onion and carrots and cook over a low heat, stirring occasionally, for 5 minutes, until softened. Add the tomatoes and cook, stirring occasionally, for a further 3 minutes.

2 Remove the pan from the heat and stir in the flour and mustard powder, then return to the heat and cook, stirring constantly, for 2 minutes. Gradually stir in the stock, a little at a time, then bring to the boil, stirring constantly. Cook, stirring constantly, for a further few minutes, until thickened.

3 Add the beef and stir to break it up. Season to taste with salt and pepper, then cover and simmer, stirring occasionally, for 45 minutes.

4 Gently stir in the peas, re-cover the pan and simmer, stirring occasionally, for a further 15 minutes. Taste and adjust the seasoning, adding salt and pepper if needed. Garnish with parsley and serve.

creamy salmon baked potatoes

ingredients

serves 4

4 baking potatoes,
    about 275 g/9¾ oz each,
    scrubbed
250 g/9 oz skinless salmon fillet
200 g/7 oz soft cheese
2–3 tbsp skimmed milk
2 tbsp chopped/snipped fresh
    herbs, such as dill or chives
60 g/2¼ oz mature Cheddar
    cheese, grated
salt and pepper

method

1 Preheat the oven to 200°C/400°F/Gas Mark 6. Prick the skins of the potatoes and place on the top shelf of the preheated oven. Bake for 50–60 minutes until the skins are crisp and the centres are soft when pierced with a sharp knife or skewer.

2 Meanwhile, bring a saucepan of water to the boil, then reduce the heat until the water is simmering gently. Add the salmon fillet to the pan and cook for 4–5 minutes (if in one piece), or until just cooked but still moist. Using a fork, flake the flesh into a bowl.

3 In a separate bowl, blend the soft cheese with just enough of the milk to loosen, then stir in the herbs and a little salt and pepper.

4 When the potatoes are cooked, preheat the grill to high. Cut the potatoes in half lengthways. Carefully scoop the potato flesh out of the skins, reserving the skins. Add to the soft cheese mixture and mash together. Lightly stir in the salmon flakes.

5 Spoon the filling into the potato skins and top with the Cheddar cheese. Cook under the preheated grill for 1–2 minutes, until the cheese is bubbling and turning golden. Serve immediately.

cauliflower cheese

ingredients

serves 4

1 cauliflower, trimmed and cut into
   florets (675 g/1 lb 8 oz
   prepared weight)
40 g/1½ oz butter
40 g/1½ oz plain flour
450 ml/16 fl oz milk
115 g/4 oz Cheddar cheese,
   finely grated
whole nutmeg, for grating
1 tbsp grated Parmesan cheese
salt and pepper

method

1 Bring a saucepan of lightly salted water to the boil,
   add the cauliflower, bring back to the boil and cook for
   4–5 minutes. It should still be firm. Drain, place in a
   warmed 1.4-litre/2½-pint gratin dish and keep warm.

2 Melt the butter in the rinsed-out pan over a
   medium heat and stir in the flour. Cook for 1 minute,
   stirring constantly.

3 Remove the pan from the heat and gradually stir in the
   milk until you have a smooth consistency.

4 Return the pan to a low heat and continue to stir while
   the sauce comes to the boil and thickens. Reduce the
   heat and simmer gently, stirring constantly, for about
   3 minutes, until the sauce is creamy and smooth.

5 Remove from the heat and stir in the Cheddar cheese
   and a good grating of the nutmeg. Taste and season
   well with salt and pepper. Meanwhile, preheat the grill
   to high.

6 Pour the hot sauce over the cauliflower, top with the
   Parmesan cheese and place under the preheated grill
   to brown. Serve immediately.

macaroni salad

ingredients

serves 6–8

225 g/8 oz dried macaroni
50 ml/2 fl oz mayonnaise,
    plus extra if needed
50 ml/2 fl oz natural yogurt
1 tbsp fresh lemon juice
½ tsp garlic salt
½ tsp pepper
40 g/1½ oz celery, diced
40 g/1½ oz spring onions,
    finely chopped
40 g/1½ oz black olives,
    finely chopped
50 g/1¼ oz tomatoes,
    finely chopped
2 tbsp chopped fresh flat-leaf
    parsley
salt and pepper

method

1 Bring a medium-sized saucepan of lightly salted water to the boil, add the macaroni and cook according to the packet instructions. Drain.

2 Meanwhile, combine the mayonnaise, yogurt, lemon juice, garlic salt and the pepper in a large bowl. Stir in the hot macaroni, then add the celery, spring onions, olives, tomatoes and parsley. Season to taste with salt and pepper and add more mayonnaise if it seems dry, then leave to cool completely.

3 Cover with clingfilm and chill for at least 2 hours until cold. Serve cold. The salad will keep in the refrigerator for up to 3 days.

corned beef hash

ingredients

serves 6

25 g/1 oz butter
1 tbsp vegetable oil
675 g/1 lb 8 oz corned beef,
    cut into small cubes
1 onion, diced
675 g/1 lb 8 oz potatoes,
    cut into small cubes
¼ tsp paprika
¼ tsp garlic powder
4 tbsp diced green pepper or
    jalapeño chillies
1 tbsp snipped chives, plus extra to
    garnish
salt and pepper
6 poached eggs, to serve

method

1 Put the butter, oil, corned beef and onion into a large, cold, non-stick or heavy-based frying pan. Place the pan over a medium–low heat and cook, stirring occasionally, for 10 minutes.

2 Meanwhile, bring a large saucepan of lightly salted water to the boil, add the potatoes, bring back to the boil and cook for 5–7 minutes, until partially cooked but still very firm. Drain well and add to the frying pan, together with the remaining ingredients.

3 Mix together well and press down lightly with a spatula to flatten. Increase the heat to medium. Every 10 minutes, turn the mixture with a spatula to bring the crusty base up to the top. Do this several times until the mixture is well-browned, the potatoes are crisp-edged and the cubes of meat are caramelized.

4 Taste and adjust the seasoning, if necessary. Transfer to warmed plates and top each with a poached egg. Garnish with chives and serve immediately.

fried chicken wings

ingredients

serves 4

12 chicken wings
1 egg
60 ml/ 4 tbsp milk
4 heaped tbsp plain flour
1 tsp paprika
225 g/8 oz breadcrumbs
55 g/2 oz butter
salt and pepper

method

1 Preheat the oven to 220°C/425°F/Gas Mark 7. Separate the chicken wings into three pieces each. Discard the bony tip. Beat the egg with the milk in a shallow dish. Combine the flour, paprika, and salt and pepper to taste in a separate shallow dish. Place the breadcrumbs in another shallow dish.

2 Dip the chicken pieces into the egg to coat well, then drain and roll in the seasoned flour. Remove, shaking off any excess, then roll the chicken in the bread-crumbs, gently pressing them onto the surface and shaking off any excess.

3 Put the butter in a shallow roasting tin large enough to hold all the chicken pieces in a single layer. Place the tin in the preheated oven and melt the butter. Remove from the oven and arrange the chicken, skin-side down, in the tin. Return to the oven and bake for 10 minutes. Turn and bake for a further 10 minutes, or until the chicken is tender and the juices run clear when a skewer is inserted into the thickest part of the meat.

4 Remove the chicken from the tin. Serve hot or at room temperature.

fish hash

ingredients
serves 4

2 cooked potatoes, diced
450 g/1 lb canned fish, such as
    tuna, drained and flaked, or
    350 g/12 oz leftover cooked
    fish, flaked
55 g/2 oz butter
3 tbsp single cream or milk
salt and pepper
chopped fresh parsley, to garnish

method

1 Gently mix together the potatoes and fish in a bowl
   and season to taste with salt and pepper.

2 Melt the butter in a heavy-based frying pan over a
   medium–low heat. Add the fish mixture and spread
   it out evenly, pressing down with a fish slice to crush
   the potatoes slightly. Pour the cream over the top
   and cook, occasionally shaking the pan, for about
   10 minutes, until the underside is golden.

3 Invert a plate over the pan, then, holding the plate
   and pan together, turn the hash on to the plate.
   Carefully slide it back into the pan and cook for a
   further 5–8 minutes, until the second side is golden.
   Garnish with parsley and serve immediately.

potato pancakes

ingredients

makes 12 pancakes

4 large potatoes, peeled and
    coarsely grated
1 large onion, grated
2 eggs, lightly beaten
55 g/2 oz fine matzo meal
1 tsp salt
pepper
sunflower oil, for frying

to serve

soured cream
thinly sliced smoked salmon
snipped chives

method

1 Preheat the oven to 110°C/225°F/Gas Mark ¼ and line
   a heatproof plate with kitchen paper. Working in small
   batches, put the potatoes on a tea towel, fold over
   and squeeze to extract as much water as possible.

2 Put the potatoes in a large bowl, add the onion, eggs,
   matzo meal and the salt. Add pepper to taste and
   mix together.

3 Heat a large, heavy-based frying pan over a medium–
   high heat. Add a thin layer of oil and heat until hot.
   Drop 2 tablespoons of the mixture into the pan and
   flatten slightly. Add as many more pancakes as will
   fit without overcrowding the pan. Fry for 2 minutes,
   or until crisp and golden underneath. Flip or turn
   with a palette knife and continue frying for a further
   1–2 minutes, until crisp and golden.

4 Repeat this process using the remaining batter, adding
   extra oil between batches, if necessary. Keep the
   cooked pancakes warm in the preheated oven.

5 Serve the pancakes hot, topped with soured cream
   and smoked salmon and sprinkled with chives.

variation

For a special treat, add a small spoonful of caviar or
lumpfish roe on top of the cream instead of the salmon.

fabulous
family food

barbecue-glazed drumsticks

ingredients

serves 6

12 chicken drumsticks,
    about 1.6 kg/3 lb 8 oz
225 ml/8 fl oz barbecue sauce
1 tbsp soft light brown sugar
1 tbsp cider vinegar
1 tsp salt
½ tsp pepper
½ tsp hot pepper sauce
vegetable oil, for brushing

method

1 Using a sharp knife, make two slashes, about 2.5 cm/
   1 inch apart, into the thickest part of the drumsticks,
   cutting to the bone. Put the drumsticks into a large,
   sealable polythene freezer bag.

2 Mix together 4 tablespoons of the barbecue sauce,
   the sugar, vinegar, salt, pepper and hot pepper sauce in
   a small bowl. Pour the mixture into the bag, press out
   most of the air and seal tightly. Shake the bag gently to
   distribute the sauce evenly and leave to marinate in the
   refrigerator for at least 4 hours.

3 Preheat the oven to 200°C/400°F/Gas Mark 6. Line
   a baking sheet with foil and brush lightly with oil.

4 Using tongs, transfer the drumsticks to the prepared
   baking sheet, spacing them evenly apart. Discard the
   marinade. Brush both sides of the drumsticks with
   some of the remaining barbecue sauce.

5 Bake in the preheated oven for 15 minutes, then
   remove from the oven and brush generously with
   more barbecue sauce. Return to the oven and repeat
   this process three more times for a total cooking time
   of 1 hour or until the chicken is tender and the juices
   run clear when a skewer is inserted into the thickest
   part of the meat. When done, the chicken will be
   cooked through with a thick, beautiful glaze.

tuna & pasta casserole

ingredients

serves 4–6

200 g/7 oz dried ribbon egg pasta,
such as tagliatelle
25 g/1 oz butter
55 g/2 oz fine fresh breadcrumbs
400 ml/14 fl oz canned condensed
cream of mushroom soup
125 ml/4 fl oz milk
2 celery sticks, chopped
1 red pepper, deseeded
and chopped
1 green pepper, deseeded
and chopped
140 g/5 oz mature Cheddar
cheese, coarsely grated
2 tbsp chopped fresh parsley
200 g/7 oz canned tuna in oil,
drained and flaked
salt and pepper

method

1 Preheat the oven to 200°C/400°F/Gas Mark 6. Bring a
large saucepan of lightly salted water to the boil. Add
the pasta, bring back to the boil and cook for 2 minutes
less than specified on the packet instructions.

2 Meanwhile, melt the butter in a separate small
saucepan. Stir in the breadcrumbs, then remove from
the heat and set aside.

3 Drain the pasta well and set aside. Pour the soup into
the pasta pan, set over a medium heat, then stir in the
milk, celery, red pepper, green pepper, half the cheese
and all the parsley.

4 Add the tuna and gently stir in so that the flakes don't
break up. Season to taste with salt and pepper. Heat
just until small bubbles appear around the edge of the
mixture – do not boil.

5 Stir the pasta into the pan and use two forks to mix all
the ingredients together. Spoon the mixture into an
ovenproof dish that is also suitable for serving and
spread it out.

6 Stir the remaining cheese into the buttered breadcrumbs, then sprinkle over the top of the pasta mixture.
Bake in the preheated oven for 20–25 minutes, until
the topping is golden. Remove from the oven, then
leave to stand for 5 minutes before serving straight
from the dish.

chicken pot pies

ingredients

serves 6

1 tbsp olive oil

225 g/8 oz button mushrooms, sliced

1 onion, finely chopped

350 g/12 oz carrots, sliced

115 g/4 oz celery, sliced

1 litre/1¾ pints chicken stock

85 g/3 oz butter

55 g/2 oz plain flour, plus extra for dusting

900 g/2 lb skinless, boneless chicken breasts, cut into 2.5-cm/1-inch cubes

115 g/4 oz frozen peas

1 tsp chopped fresh thyme or a pinch of dried thyme

675 g/1 lb 8 oz shortcrust pastry, thawed, if frozen

1 egg, lightly beaten

salt and pepper

method

1 Heat the oil in a large saucepan and fry the mushrooms and onion gently until golden. Add the carrots, celery and half the stock and simmer for 12–15 minutes, until the vegetables are almost tender.

2 Melt the butter in another large saucepan over a medium heat. Whisk in the flour and cook, stirring constantly, for 4 minutes. Gradually whisk in the remaining chicken stock. Reduce the heat and simmer, stirring, until thickened.

3 Stir in the vegetables, chicken, peas and thyme and season with salt and pepper. Simmer, stirring constantly, for 5 minutes. Adjust the seasoning, if necessary, and remove from the heat. Preheat the oven to 200°C/400°F/Gas Mark 6.

4 Divide the filling between six large ramekins, leaving 1 cm/½ inch at the top. Roll out the pastry on a lightly floured work surface and cut out six rounds slightly larger than the ramekins. Put the rounds on top and fold over all the way around to make a rim. Cut a small cross in the centre of each.

5 Put the ramekins on a baking sheet and brush the pastry tops with the beaten egg. Bake in the preheated oven for 35–40 minutes, until golden brown and bubbling. Remove from the oven and leave to cool for 15 minutes before serving.

crab cakes with tartare sauce

ingredients

makes 6 cakes

1 large egg, beaten
2 tbsp mayonnaise
$\frac{1}{2}$ tsp Dijon mustard
$\frac{1}{4}$ tsp Worcestershire sauce
$\frac{1}{2}$ tsp celery salt
$\frac{1}{4}$ tsp salt
pinch of cayenne pepper (optional)
40 g/1$\frac{1}{2}$ oz cream crackers, finely crushed
450 g/1 lb fresh crabmeat
85–140 g/3–5 oz fresh breadcrumbs
25 g/1 oz unsalted butter
1 tbsp vegetable oil
salad leaves and lemon wedges, to serve

tartare sauce

225 ml/8 fl oz mayonnaise
4 tbsp sweet pickle relish
1 tbsp very finely chopped onion
1 tbsp chopped capers
1 tbsp chopped parsley
1$\frac{1}{2}$ tbsp freshly squeezed lemon juice
dash of Worcestershire sauce
few drops of hot pepper sauce (optional)
salt and pepper

method

1 To make the crab cakes, whisk together the egg, mayonnaise, mustard, Worcestershire sauce, celery salt, salt and cayenne pepper, if using, in a large bowl until combined. Stir in the cracker crumbs with a spatula, then leave to stand for 5 minutes.

2 Pick over the crabmeat to remove any pieces of shell or cartilage, then gently fold into the mixture, trying to avoid breaking it up too much. Cover the bowl with clingfilm and chill in the refrigerator for at least 1 hour.

3 Meanwhile, make the tartare sauce. Mix together all the ingredients in a bowl and season to taste with salt and pepper. Cover and chill in the refrigerator for at least 1 hour before serving.

4 Sprinkle the breadcrumbs over a large plate until lightly covered. Shape the crab mixture into six even-sized cakes, about 2.5 cm/1 inch thick, placing them on the plate as they are formed. Dust the tops of each crab cake lightly with more breadcrumbs.

5 Melt the butter with the oil in a large frying pan over a medium–high heat. Carefully transfer each crab cake from the plate to the pan using a metal spatula.

6 Cook the crab cakes for 4 minutes on each side, until golden brown. Remove from the pan and drain on kitchen paper. Serve immediately with the tartare sauce, salad leaves and lemon wedges.

pizza margherita

ingredients

serves 6

pizza dough

15 g/¹/₂ oz easy-blend dried yeast

1 tsp sugar

250 ml/9 fl oz lukewarm water

350 g/12 oz strong white flour,
plus extra for dusting

1 tsp salt

1 tbsp olive oil, plus extra for oiling

topping

400 g/14 oz canned chopped
tomatoes

2 garlic cloves, crushed

2 tsp dried basil

1 tbsp olive oil

2 tbsp tomato purée

100 g/3¹/₂ oz mozzarella cheese,
chopped

2 tbsp freshly grated Parmesan
cheese

salt and pepper

fresh basil leaves, to garnish

method

1 Place the yeast and sugar in a measuring jug and mix with 50 ml/2 fl oz of the water. Leave the yeast mixture in a warm place for 15 minutes or until frothy.

2 Mix the flour with the salt and make a well in the centre. Add the oil, the yeast mixture and the remaining water. Using a wooden spoon, mix to form a smooth dough. Turn out the dough onto a floured work surface and knead for 4–5 minutes or until smooth. Return the dough to the bowl, cover with a sheet of oiled clingfilm and leave to rise for 30 minutes, or until doubled in size.

3 Knead the dough for 2 minutes. Stretch the dough with your hands or roll out on a floured surface with a rolling pin, then place it on an oiled baking tray. The dough should be no more than 5 mm/¹/₄ inch thick.

4 Preheat the oven to 200°C/400°F/Gas Mark 6. To make the topping, place the tomatoes, garlic, basil, oil, and salt and pepper to taste in a large frying pan over a medium heat and leave to simmer for 20 minutes or until the sauce has thickened. Stir in the tomato purée and leave to cool slightly.

5 Spread the topping evenly over the pizza base. Top with the mozzarella cheese and Parmesan cheese and bake in the preheated oven for 20–25 minutes. Serve hot, garnished with basil leaves.

fish cakes

ingredients

serves 4

450 g/1 lb floury potatoes,
    cut into chunks
450 g/1 lb mixed fish fillets, such
    as cod and salmon, skinned
2 tbsp chopped fresh tarragon
grated rind of 1 lemon
2 tbsp double cream
1 tbsp plain flour
1 egg, beaten
115 g/4 oz breadcrumbs, made
    from day-old white or
    wholemeal bread
4 tbsp vegetable oil,
    for shallow-frying
salt and pepper
watercress and lemon wedges,
    to serve

method

1 Cook the potatoes in a large saucepan of boiling salted water for 15–20 minutes. Drain well and mash with a potato masher until smooth.

2 Meanwhile, put the fish in a frying pan and just cover with water. Place over a medium heat and bring to the boil, then reduce the heat, cover and simmer gently for 5 minutes, until cooked.

3 Remove from the heat and drain the fish on to a plate. When cool enough to handle, flake the fish into large chunks, ensuring that there are no bones.

4 Mix the potatoes with the fish, tarragon, lemon rind and cream. Season well with salt and pepper and shape into 4 large patties or 8 smaller ones.

5 Dust the patties with flour and dip them into the beaten egg. Coat thoroughly in the breadcrumbs. Place on a baking tray and leave to chill in the refrigerator for at least 30 minutes.

6 Heat the oil in the frying pan and fry the patties over a medium heat for 5 minutes on each side, turning them carefully using a palette knife or a fish slice.

7 Serve with the watercress, accompanied by lemon wedges for squeezing over the fish cakes.

roast butternut squash

ingredients
serves 4

1 butternut squash,
about 450 g/1 lb
1 onion, chopped
2–3 garlic cloves, crushed
4 small tomatoes, chopped
85 g/3 oz chestnut mushrooms,
chopped
85 g/3 oz canned butter beans,
drained, rinsed and roughly
chopped
1 courgette, about 115 g/4 oz,
grated
1 tbsp chopped fresh oregano, plus
extra, to garnish
2 tbsp tomato purée
300 ml/10 fl oz water
4 spring onions, chopped
1 tbsp Worcestershire sauce,
or to taste
pepper

method

1 Preheat the oven to 190°C/375°F/Gas Mark 5. Prick the squash all over with a metal skewer then roast for 40 minutes, or until tender. Remove from the oven and leave to rest until cool enough to handle.

2 Cut the squash in half, scoop out and discard the seeds, then scoop out some of the flesh, making hollows in both halves. Chop the scooped-out flesh and put in a bowl. Place the two squash halves side by side in a large roasting tin.

3 Add the onion, garlic, tomatoes and mushrooms to the squash flesh in the bowl. Add the butter beans, courgette, oregano and pepper to taste and mix well. Spoon the filling into the two halves of the squash, packing it down as firmly as possible.

4 Mix the tomato purée with the water, spring onions and Worcestershire sauce in a small bowl and pour over the squash.

5 Cover loosely with a large sheet of foil and bake for 30 minutes, or until piping hot. Serve in warmed bowls, garnished with some chopped oregano.

meatloaf

ingredients

serves 6–8

100 g/3¹/₂ oz carrots, diced
55 g/2 oz celery, diced
1 onion, diced
1 red pepper, deseeded and
    chopped
4 large white mushrooms, sliced
25 g/1 oz butter
1 tbsp olive oil, plus extra for
    brushing
3 garlic cloves, crushed
1 tsp dried thyme
2 tsp finely chopped rosemary
1 tsp Worcestershire sauce
4 tbsp tomato ketchup
¹/₄ tsp cayenne pepper
1.1 kg/2 lb 8 oz beef mince, chilled
2 tsp salt
1 tsp pepper
2 eggs, beaten
55 g/2 oz fresh breadcrumbs
garden peas and Perfect Mash
    (see page 102), to serve

glaze

2 tbsp brown sugar
2 tbsp tomato ketchup
1 tbsp Dijon mustard
salt

method

1 Put the vegetables into a food processor and pulse
until very finely chopped. Melt the butter with the oil
and garlic in a large frying pan. Add the vegetable
mixture and cook over a medium heat, stirring
frequently, for about 10 minutes. Remove the pan from
the heat and stir in the thyme, rosemary, Worcestershire
sauce, tomato ketchup and cayenne pepper. Leave to
cool to room temperature.

2 Preheat the oven to 160°C/325°F/Gas Mark 3. Lightly
brush a shallow roasting tin with olive oil.

3 Put the beef into a large bowl and gently break it up
with your fingertips. Add the cooled vegetable mixture,
salt, pepper and eggs and mix gently. Add the
breadcrumbs and mix to combine. The less you work
the meat, the better the final texture.

4 Put the meatloaf mixture in the centre of the
prepared roasting tin and shape it into a loaf about
15 cm/6 inches wide by 10 cm/4 inches high. Bake in
the preheated oven for 30 minutes.

5 To make the glaze, whisk together all the ingredients
with a pinch of salt in a small bowl.

6 Remove the meatloaf from the oven and spread
the glaze over the top and sides. Bake for a further
15 minutes. Slice thickly and serve with peas and mash.

spaghetti & meatballs

ingredients

serves 4

2 tbsp olive oil, plus extra for brushing

1 onion, finely diced

4 garlic cloves, finely chopped

½ tsp dried Italian herbs

140 g/5 oz fresh fine breadcrumbs

4 tbsp milk

900 g/2 lb beef mince, well chilled

2 large eggs, lightly beaten

5 tbsp chopped fresh flat-leaf parsley

55 g/2 oz Parmesan cheese, grated, plus extra to serve

1.5 litres/ 2¾ pints marinara or other ready-made pasta sauce

225 ml/8 fl oz water

450 g/1 lb thick dried spaghetti

salt and pepper

method

1 Heat the oil in a saucepan and gently cook the onion, garlic and a pinch of salt for 6-7 minutes until softened and golden. Remove from the heat, stir in the herbs and leave to cool.

2 Put the breadcrumbs into a bowl, toss with the milk and leave to soak for 10 minutes. Preheat the oven to 220°C/425°F/Gas Mark 7. Brush a baking sheet with oil.

3 Put the beef, eggs, parsley, cheese, breadcrumbs, cooled onion mixture, salt and pepper to taste, into a bowl. Mix well with your hands until thoroughly combined.

4 Roll the mixture into balls about the size of a golf ball. Put them on the prepared tray and bake in the oven for 20 minutes. Heat the pasta sauce and the water in a saucepan. When the meatballs are done, add them to the hot sauce, reduce the heat to very low, cover and simmer gently for 45 minutes.

5 Cook the spaghetti according to the packet instructions, until tender but still firm to the bite. Drain in a colander and tip into a large serving dish. Ladle some of the sauce from the meatballs over it and toss to coat. Top with the meatballs and the remaining sauce, sprinkle with cheese and serve immediately.

home-made burgers

ingredients
makes 6 burgers

1 kg/2 lb 4 oz beef mince
1 small onion, grated
1 tbsp chopped fresh parsley
2 tsp Worcestershire sauce
2 tbsp sunflower oil
salt and pepper

to serve

6 burger buns, split and toasted
lettuce leaves
tomato slices
gherkins, sliced
tomato ketchup

method

1 Put the beef, onion and parsley into a bowl and add the Worcestershire sauce. Season to taste with salt and pepper and mix well with your hands until thoroughly combined.

2 Divide the mixture into six equal portions and shape into balls, then gently flatten into patties. If you have time, chill in the refrigerator for 30 minutes to firm up.

3 Heat the oil in a large frying pan. Add the burgers, in batches, and cook over a medium heat for 5–8 minutes on each side, turning them carefully with a fish slice. Remove from the pan and keep warm while you cook the remaining burgers.

4 Serve in toasted buns with lettuce leaves, tomato slices, gherkins and tomato ketchup.

lasagne

ingredients

serves 6

2 tbsp olive oil
500 g/1 lb 2 oz fresh beef
    mince
1 onion, chopped
1 garlic clove, finely chopped
1 carrot, diced
1 tbsp chopped fresh flat-leaf
    parsley
6 fresh basil leaves, torn
600 ml/1 pint passata
550 g/1 lb 4 oz ricotta cheese
1 egg, lightly beaten
8 no pre-cook lasagne sheets
225 g/8 oz mozzarella cheese,
    grated
salt and pepper

method

1 Heat the oil in a saucepan. Add the beef, onion, garlic and carrot and cook over a medium heat, stirring frequently and breaking up the meat with a wooden spoon, for 5–8 minutes, until the beef is evenly browned.

2 Stir in the herbs, season to taste with salt and pepper and pour in the passata. Bring to the boil, then reduce the heat, cover and simmer for 15 minutes.

3 Meanwhile, preheat the oven to 190°C/375°F/Gas Mark 5. Mix the ricotta with the egg, stirring until smooth and thoroughly combined.

4 Make alternating layers of the beef mixture, lasagne sheets, ricotta mixture and mozzarella in an ovenproof dish, ending with a layer of mozzarella. Bake in the preheated oven for 40–45 minutes, until the topping is golden and bubbling. Leave to stand for 5 minutes before serving.

old-fashioned chicken stew

ingredients

serves 6

2 tbsp vegetable oil

1 x 1.8–2.25-kg/4–5-lb chicken, cut into quarters

700 ml/1¼ pints chicken stock

700 ml/1¼ pints water

4 garlic cloves, peeled

1 bay leaf

4 fresh thyme sprigs

70 g/2½ oz butter

2 carrots, cut into 1-cm/½-inch lengths

2 celery sticks, cut into 1-cm/½-inch lengths

1 large onion, chopped

5 tbsp plain flour

1½ tsp salt

pepper

dash of hot pepper sauce

dumplings

200 g/7 oz plain flour

1 tsp salt

2 tsp baking powder

¼ tsp bicarbonate of soda

40 g/1½ oz butter, chilled

2 tbsp thinly sliced spring onions

60 ml/4 tbsp buttermilk

175 ml/6 fl oz milk

method

1 Heat the oil in a large casserole, add the chicken pieces and brown all over. Add the stock, water, garlic, bay leaf and thyme then cover and simmer for 30 minutes. Remove the chicken and leave to cool. Strain the cooking liquid, skimming off any fat.

2 Put the butter, carrots, celery and onion into the casserole and cook for 5 minutes. Stir in the flour and cook, stirring constantly, for 2 minutes. Gradually whisk in the reserved cooking liquid. Add the salt, pepper and the hot pepper sauce. Cover and simmer for 30 minutes, until the vegetables are tender.

3 Skin the chicken pieces and tear the meat into chunks. Stir the chunks into the cooked vegetables, cover the casserole and reduce the heat to low.

4 To make the dumplings, sift the flour, salt, baking powder and bicarbonate of soda together into a bowl. Rub in the butter until the mixture resembles coarse breadcrumbs. Add the spring onions, buttermilk and milk and mix into a thick dough.

5 Increase the heat under the casserole to medium and stir well. Shape the dough into large balls and add to the casserole. Cover and simmer for 15 minutes, until the dumplings are firm and cooked in the middle. Serve immediately.

hearty beef stew

ingredients

serves 4

1.3 kg/3 lb boneless braising steak,
   cut into 5-cm/2-inch pieces
2 tbsp vegetable oil
2 onions, cut into 2.5-cm/1-inch
   pieces
3 tbsp plain flour
3 garlic cloves, finely chopped
1 litre/1¾ pints beef stock,
   plus extra if needed
3 carrots, sliced
2 celery sticks, cut into
   2.5-cm/1-inch lengths
1 tbsp tomato ketchup
1 bay leaf
¼ tsp dried thyme
¼ tsp dried rosemary
900 g/2 lb Maris Piper potatoes,
   cut into large chunks
salt and pepper

method

1 Season the steak very generously with salt and pepper.
   Heat the oil in a large flameproof casserole over a high
   heat. When the oil begins to smoke slightly, add the
   steak, in batches, if necessary, and cook, stirring
   frequently, for 5–8 minutes, until well browned. Using
   a slotted spoon, transfer to a bowl.

2 Reduce the heat to medium, add the onions to the
   casserole and cook, stirring occasionally, for 5 minutes,
   until translucent. Stir in the flour and cook, stirring
   constantly, for 2 minutes. Add the garlic and cook for
   1 minute. Whisk in 225 ml/8 fl oz of the stock and cook,
   scraping up all the sediment from the base of the
   casserole, then stir in the remaining stock. Add the
   carrots, celery, tomato ketchup, bay leaf, thyme,
   rosemary and 1 teaspoon of salt. Return the steak to
   the casserole.

3 Bring back to a gentle simmer, cover and cook over a
   low heat for 1 hour. Add the potatoes, re-cover the
   casserole and simmer for a further 30 minutes. Remove
   the lid, increase the heat to medium and cook, stirring
   occasionally, for a further 30 minutes, or until the meat
   and vegetables are tender.

4 If the stew becomes too thick, add a little more stock
   or water and adjust the seasoning, if necessary. Leave
   to stand for 15 minutes before serving.

pork chops with apple sauce

ingredients

serves 4

4 pork rib chops on the bone, each
   about 3 cm/1¼ inches thick,
   at room temperature

1½ tbsp sunflower oil or
   rapeseed oil

salt and pepper

apple sauce

450 g/1 lb cooking apples, such as
   bramley, peeled, cored and
   diced

4 tbsp caster sugar, plus extra,
   if needed

finely grated zest of ½ lemon

½ tbsp lemon juice, plus extra,
   if needed

4 tbsp water

¼ tsp ground cinnamon

knob of butter

method

1 To make the apple sauce, put the apples, sugar,
   lemon zest, lemon juice and water into a heavy-based
   saucepan over a high heat and bring to the boil, stirring
   to dissolve the sugar. Reduce the heat to low, cover and
   simmer for 15–20 minutes, until the apples are tender
   and fall apart when you mash them against the side
   of the pan. Stir in the cinnamon and butter and beat
   the apples until they are as smooth or chunky as
   you like. Stir in extra sugar or lemon juice, to taste.
   Remove the pan from the heat, cover and keep the
   apple sauce warm.

2 Meanwhile, preheat the oven to 200°C/400°F/Gas
   Mark 6. Pat the chops dry and season to taste with salt
   and pepper. Heat the oil in a large ovenproof frying
   pan over a medium–high heat. Add the chops and fry
   for 3 minutes on each side to brown.

3 Transfer the pan to the oven and roast the chops
   for 7–9 minutes until cooked through and the juices
   run clear when you cut the chops. Remove the pan
   from the oven, cover with foil and leave to stand for
   3 minutes. Gently reheat the apple sauce, if necessary.

4 Transfer the chops to warmed plates and spoon over
   the pan juices. Serve immediately, accompanied by the
   apple sauce.

steak & chips

ingredients

serves 4

4 sirloin steaks, about 225 g/
    8 oz each
4 tsp hot pepper sauce
salt and pepper

chips

450 g/1 lb potatoes
2 tbsp sunflower oil

watercress butter

1 bunch of watercress
85 g/3 oz unsalted butter, softened

method

1 To make the chips, preheat the oven to 200°C/400°F/ Gas Mark 6. Cut the potatoes into thick, even-sized chips. Rinse them under cold running water and then dry well on a clean tea towel. Place in a bowl, add the oil and toss together until coated.

2 Spread the chips on a baking sheet and cook in the preheated oven for 40–45 minutes, turning once, until golden.

3 To make the watercress butter, finely chop enough watercress to fill 4 tablespoons. Place the butter in a small bowl and beat in the chopped watercress with a fork until fully incorporated. Cover with clingfilm and leave to chill in the refrigerator until required.

4 Preheat a griddle pan to high. Sprinkle each steak with 1 teaspoon of the hot pepper sauce, rubbing it in well. Season to taste with salt and pepper.

5 Cook the steaks in the preheated pan for 2½ minutes each side for rare, 4 minutes each side for medium and 6 minutes each side for well done. Transfer to serving plates and serve immediately, topped with the watercress butter and accompanied by the chips.

turkey & stuffing

ingredients
serves 8–10

4.5-kg/10-lb oven-ready turkey,
 wiped and patted dry
2 garlic cloves, sliced
1 orange, sliced
4 tbsp butter, melted, for brushing
salt and pepper

stuffing

450 g/1 lb spicy sausage meat
55 g/2 oz butter, plus extra for
 greasing
3 celery sticks, finely chopped
1 onion, finely chopped
6 slices day-old bread, crusts
 removed and cubed
125 ml/4 fl oz turkey stock or
 vegetable stock, plus extra if
 needed
150 g/5½ oz dried fruit, such as
 currants, sultanas and raisins
140 g/5 oz fresh cranberries,
 roughly chopped
15 g/½ oz fresh parsley,
 finely chopped
2 tsp dried thyme
1 tsp dried sage
finely grated zest and juice of
 2 large oranges
salt and pepper

method

1 To make the stuffing, put the sausage into a frying pan over a medium–high heat and cook until coloured. Remove the meat and pour off the fat. Melt the butter in the pan, add the celery and onion and fry, stirring, until softened. Add the bread and stir until it starts to colour, then add the contents of the pan to the sausage. Stir in the stock, dried fruit, cranberries, herbs and orange zest. Add enough orange juice to make a moist stuffing and season to taste.

2 Preheat the oven to 180°C/350°F/Gas Mark 4. Use enough stuffing to fill the neck end of the turkey, securing the skin with wooden cocktail sticks. Put the garlic and orange slices into the cavity and truss the legs together. Put any leftover stuffing in a greased oven dish and cover with foil.

3 Weigh the stuffed bird and calculate the cooking time at 20 minutes per 450 g/1 pound plus 20 minutes. Place the bird, breast side up, on a roasting rack in a roasting tin, smear with butter and season to taste with salt and pepper. Cover loosely with foil and roast for the calculated time, or until the juices run clear when a skewer is inserted into the thickest part of the meat.

4 Remove the turkey from the oven, cover and let rest, for 30–45 minutes. Roast the extra stuffing for 20–25 minutes. Carve the turkey and serve with the stuffing.

roast gammon

ingredients

serves 6

1.3 kg/3 lb boneless gammon,
    pre-soaked if necessary
2 tbsp Dijon mustard
85 g/3 oz demerara sugar
½ tsp ground cinnamon
½ tsp ground ginger
18 whole cloves
ready-made Cumberland sauce,
    to serve

method

1 Place the gammon in a large saucepan, cover with cold
    water and slowly bring to the boil over a gentle heat.
    Cover the pan and simmer very gently for 1 hour.

2 Preheat the oven to 200°C/400°F/Gas Mark 6.

3 Remove the gammon from the pan and drain. Remove
    the rind from the gammon and discard. Score the fat
    into a diamond-shaped pattern with a sharp knife.

4 Spread the mustard over the fat. Mix the sugar and
    the ground spices together on a large plate and roll the
    gammon in the mixture, pressing down well to
    coat evenly.

5 Stud the diamond shapes with cloves and place the
    joint in a roasting tin. Roast in the preheated oven for
    20 minutes, until the glaze is a rich golden colour.

6 To serve hot, leave to stand for 20 minutes before
    carving. If the gammon is to be served cold, it can be
    cooked a day ahead. Serve with Cumberland sauce.

leg of lamb pot roast

ingredients

serves 4

1 leg of lamb, weighing 1.6 kg/
   3 lb 8 oz
3–4 fresh rosemary sprigs
115 g/4 oz streaky bacon rashers
4 tbsp olive oil
2–3 garlic cloves, crushed
2 onions, sliced
2 carrots, sliced
2 celery sticks, sliced
300 ml/10 fl oz dry white wine
1 tbsp tomato purée
300 ml/10 fl oz lamb stock or
   chicken stock
3 tomatoes, peeled, quartered
   and deseeded
1 tbsp chopped fresh parsley
1 tbsp chopped fresh oregano
   or marjoram
salt and pepper
fresh rosemary sprigs, to garnish

method

1 Wipe the lamb all over with kitchen paper, trim off any excess fat and season to taste with salt and pepper, rubbing in well. Lay the sprigs of rosemary over the lamb, cover evenly with the bacon and tie in place securely with some kitchen string.

2 Heat the oil in a large frying pan over a medium heat, add the lamb and fry for 10 minutes, turning several times. Remove from the pan.

3 Preheat the oven to 160°C/325°F/Gas Mark 3. Transfer the oil from the pan to a large, flameproof casserole, add the garlic and onions and cook for 3–4 minutes, until the onions are beginning to soften. Add the carrots and celery and cook for a further few minutes.

4 Lay the lamb on top of the vegetables. Pour the wine over the lamb, add the tomato purée and simmer for 3–4 minutes. Add the stock, tomatoes and herbs and season to taste with salt and pepper. Bring back to the boil and cook for a further 3–4 minutes.

5 Lightly cover the casserole and cook in the preheated oven for 2–2½ hours until very tender.

6 Remove the lamb from the casserole and keep warm. Strain the juices, skimming off any fat. Garnish the lamb with sprigs of rosemary and serve with the vegetables and juices.

roast chicken

ingredients

serves 6

2.25 kg/5 lb free-range chicken
55 g/2 oz butter
2 tbsp chopped fresh lemon thyme
1 lemon, quartered
125 ml/4 fl oz white wine,
    plus extra if needed
salt and pepper
roasted vegetables, to serve

method

1 Preheat the oven to 220°C/425°F/Gas Mark 7. Make sure the chicken is clean, wiping it inside and out with kitchen paper, then place in a roasting tin.

2 In a bowl, soften the butter with a fork, mix in the thyme and season well with salt and pepper. Butter the chicken all over with the herb butter, inside and out, and place the lemon pieces inside the body cavity. Pour the wine over the chicken.

3 Roast in the centre of the preheated oven for 20 minutes. Reduce the temperature to 190°C/375°F/Gas Mark 5 and continue to roast for a further 1¼ hours, basting frequently. Cover with foil if the skin begins to brown too much. If the liquid in the tin dries out, add a little more wine or water.

4 Test that the chicken is cooked by piercing the thickest part of the leg with a sharp knife or skewer and making sure the juices run clear. Remove from the oven.

5 Place the chicken on a warmed serving plate, cover with foil and leave to rest for 10 minutes before carving.

6 Place the roasting tin on the hob and bubble the pan juices gently over a low heat, until they have reduced and are thick and glossy. Season to taste with salt and pepper. Serve the chicken with the pan juices and roasted vegetables.

whole roast rib of beef

ingredients

serves 6

olive oil, for rubbing
3-kg/6 lb 8-oz joint of well-hung
    rib of beef on the bone
½ tbsp plain flour
200 ml/7 fl oz strong beef stock
200 ml/7 fl oz red wine
salt and pepper

to serve

mini Yorkshire puddings,
    see page 106
roast potatoes, see page 100
glazed carrots
steamed broccoli
horseradish sauce (optional)
mustard (optional)

method

1 Preheat the oven to 220°C/425°F/Gas Mark 7.

2 Rub a generous amount of olive oil and salt and
   pepper into the beef, then place in a roasting tin.
   Transfer to the preheated oven and roast for
   30 minutes.

3 Reduce the temperature to 160°C/325°F/Gas Mark 3
   and roast for a further 60 minutes. Remove the beef
   from the oven. Cover the beef with foil and leave to
   rest for at least 30 minutes.

4 Meanwhile, make the gravy. Remove the beef from
   the tin and stir the flour into the leftover juices. Add
   the stock and wine, then simmer over a medium heat
   until reduced by about half. Strain into a jug.

5 Cut the rib bones off the meat and carve the beef.
   Serve with the gravy, Yorkshire puddings, roast
   potatoes, carrots, broccoli, horseradish sauce and
   mustard, if liked.

poached salmon

ingredients

serves 6

1 whole salmon (head on), about
   2.7 kg/6 lb to 3.6 kg/8 lb
   prepared weight
3 tbsp salt
3 bay leaves
10 black peppercorns
1 onion, peeled and sliced
1 lemon, sliced
lemon wedges, to serve

method

1 Wipe the salmon thoroughly inside and out with kitchen paper, then use the back of a cook's knife to remove any scales that might still be on the skin. Remove the fins with a pair of scissors and trim the tail. Some people prefer to cut off the head but it is traditionally served with it on.

2 Place the salmon on the two-handled rack that comes with a fish kettle, then place it in the kettle. Fill the kettle with enough cold water to cover the salmon adequately. Sprinkle over the salt, bay leaves and peppercorns and scatter in the onion and lemon slices.

3 Place the kettle over a low heat, over two burners, and bring just to the boil very slowly.

4 Cover and simmer very gently for 6–8 minutes. Leave to stand in the hot water for 15 minutes then remove the fish carefully. Serve with lemon wedges for squeezing over.

variation

To serve cold, simmer for 2 minutes only, remove from the heat and leave to cool in the water for about 2 hours with the lid on. Remove the skin when cool and decorate with slices of cucumber.

something
on the side

roast vegetables

ingredients

serves 4–6

3 parsnips, cut into 5-cm/2-inch
    chunks
4 baby turnips, cut into quarters
3 carrots, cut into 5-cm/2-inch
    chunks
450 g/1 lb butternut squash,
    peeled and cut into
    5-cm/2-inch chunks
450 g/1 lb sweet potatoes, peeled
    and cut into 5-cm/2-inch
    chunks
2 garlic cloves, finely chopped
2 tbsp chopped fresh rosemary
2 tbsp chopped fresh thyme
2 tsp chopped fresh sage
3 tbsp olive oil
salt and pepper
2 tbsp chopped fresh mixed herbs,
    such as parsley, thyme and
    mint, to garnish

method

1 Preheat the oven to 220°C/425°F/Gas Mark 7.

2 Arrange all the vegetables in a single layer in a large
   roasting tin. Scatter over the garlic and the herbs. Pour
   over the oil and season well with salt and pepper.

3 Toss all the ingredients together until they are well
   mixed and coated with the oil (you can leave them to
   marinate at this stage to allow the flavours to be
   absorbed).

4 Roast the vegetables at the top of the preheated
   oven for 50–60 minutes until they are cooked and
   nicely browned. Turn the vegetables over halfway
   through the cooking time.

5 Serve with a good handful of fresh herbs scattered on
   top and a final sprinkling of salt and pepper to taste.

sweet & sour red cabbage

ingredients

serves 6–8

1 red cabbage, about
    750 g/1 lb 10 oz
2 tbsp olive oil
2 onions, finely sliced
1 garlic clove, chopped
2 small cooking apples, peeled,
    cored and sliced
2 tbsp muscovado sugar
½ tsp ground cinnamon
1 tsp crushed juniper berries
whole nutmeg, for grating
2 tbsp red wine vinegar
grated rind and juice of 1 orange
2 tbsp redcurrant jelly
salt and pepper

method

1 Cut the cabbage into quarters, remove the centre stalk and finely shred the leaves.

2 Heat the oil in a large saucepan over a medium heat and add the cabbage, onions, garlic and apples. Stir in the sugar, cinnamon and juniper berries and grate a quarter of the nutmeg into the pan.

3 Pour over the vinegar and orange juice and add the orange rind.

4 Stir well and season to taste with salt and pepper. The pan will be quite full but the volume of the cabbage will reduce during cooking.

5 Cook over a medium heat, stirring occasionally, until the cabbage is just tender but still has 'bite'. This will take 10–15 minutes, depending on how finely the cabbage is sliced.

6 Stir in the redcurrant jelly, then taste and adjust the seasoning, adding salt and pepper if necessary. Serve immediately.

courgette fritters

ingredients
makes 20–30 fritters

100 g/3½ oz self-raising flour
2 eggs, beaten
50 ml/2 fl oz milk
300 g/10½ oz courgettes
2 tbsp fresh thyme, plus extra to
    garnish
1 tbsp oil
salt and pepper

method

1 Preheat the oven to 140°C/275°F/Gas Mark 1.

2 Sift the flour into a large bowl and make a well in the centre. Add the eggs to the well and, using a wooden spoon, gradually draw in the flour. Slowly add the milk to the mixture, stirring constantly to form a thick batter.

3 Meanwhile, grate the courgettes over a sheet of kitchen paper placed in a bowl to absorb some of the juices.

4 Add the courgettes, thyme and salt and pepper, to taste, to the batter and mix thoroughly, for about a minute.

5 Heat the oil in a large, heavy-based frying pan. Taking a tablespoon of the batter for a medium-sized fritter or half a tablespoon of batter for a smaller-sized fritter, spoon the mixture into the hot oil and cook, in batches, for 3–4 minutes on each side.

6 Remove the fritters with a slotted spoon and drain thoroughly on absorbent kitchen paper. Keep each batch warm in the oven while making the rest. Transfer to serving plates, garnish with the thyme and serve immediately.

brussels sprouts with chestnuts

ingredients

serves 4

350 g/12 oz brussels sprouts,
    trimmed
40 g/1½ oz butter
100 g/3½ oz canned whole
    chestnuts
pinch of grated nutmeg
salt and pepper
50 g/1¼ oz flaked almonds,
    to garnish

method

1 Bring a large saucepan of lightly salted water to the
    boil. Add the sprouts, bring back to the boil and cook
    for 5 minutes. Drain thoroughly.

2 Melt the butter in a large saucepan over a medium
    heat. Add the sprouts and cook, stirring, for 3 minutes,
    then add the chestnuts and nutmeg to the pan.

3 Season to taste with salt and pepper and stir well.
    Cook for a further 2 minutes, stirring, then remove
    from the heat.

4 Transfer to a warmed serving dish, scatter over the
    almonds and serve.

asparagus with lemon butter sauce

ingredients

serves 4

800 g/1 lb 12 oz asparagus spears, trimmed
1 tbsp olive oil
salt and pepper

lemon butter sauce

juice of ½ lemon
2 tbsp water
100 g/3½ oz butter, cut into cubes
pepper

method

1 Preheat the oven to 200°C/400°F/Gas Mark 6.

2 Lay the asparagus spears in a single layer on a large baking sheet. Drizzle over the oil, season to taste with salt and pepper and roast in the preheated oven for 10 minutes, or until just tender.

3 Meanwhile, make the lemon butter sauce. Pour the lemon juice into a saucepan and add the water. Heat for a minute or so, then slowly add the butter, cube by cube, stirring constantly until it has all been incorporated. Season to taste with pepper and serve warm with the asparagus.

roast potatoes

ingredients

serves 6

1.3 kg/3 lb large floury potatoes, such as King Edward, Maris Piper or Desirée, cut into even-sized chunks
3 tbsp dripping, goose fat, duck fat or olive oil
salt

method

1 Preheat the oven to 220°C/425°F/Gas Mark 7.

2 Bring a large saucepan of lightly salted water to the boil, add the potatoes, bring back to the boil and cook for 5–7 minutes. The potatoes should still be firm. Remove from the heat.

3 Meanwhile, add the dripping to a roasting tin and place the tin in the preheated oven.

4 Drain the potatoes well and return them to the saucepan. Cover with the lid and firmly shake the pan so that the surface of the potatoes is roughened to help give a much crisper texture.

5 Remove the roasting tin from the oven and carefully tip the potatoes into the hot fat. Baste them to ensure they are all coated with the fat.

6 Roast at the top of the oven for 45–50 minutes until they are browned all over and thoroughly crisp. Turn the potatoes and baste again only once during the process or the crunchy edges will be destroyed.

7 Carefully transfer the potatoes from the roasting tin into a warmed serving dish. Sprinkle with a little salt and serve immediately.

perfect mash

ingredients

serves 4

900 g/2 lb floury potatoes, such as
   King Edward, Maris Piper or
   Desirée, cut into even-sized
   chunks
55 g/2 oz butter
3 tbsp hot milk
salt and pepper

method

1 Bring a large saucepan of lightly salted water to the boil, add the potatoes, bring back to the boil and cook for 20–25 minutes until they are tender. Test with the point of a knife, but do make sure you test right to the middle to avoid lumps.

2 Remove the pan from the heat and drain the potatoes. Return the potatoes to the hot pan and mash with a potato masher until smooth.

3 Add the butter and continue to mash until it is all mixed in, then add the milk (it is better hot because the potatoes absorb it more quickly to produce a creamier mash).

4 Taste the mash and season with salt and pepper as necessary. Serve immediately.

dauphinoise potatoes

ingredients

serves 8

15 g/½ oz butter, plus extra for greasing
1 tbsp plain flour
225 ml/8 fl oz double cream
450 ml/16 fl oz milk
1 tsp salt
pinch of freshly grated nutmeg
pinch of freshly ground white pepper
4 fresh thyme sprigs
2 garlic cloves, finely chopped
2 kg/4 lb 8 oz baking potatoes, thinly sliced
115 g/4 oz gruyère cheese or white cheddar cheese, grated
salt and pepper

method

1 Preheat the oven to 190°C/375°F/Gas Mark 5. Grease a 38 x 25-cm/15 x 10-inch ovenproof dish.

2 Melt the butter in a saucepan over a medium heat. Stir in the flour and cook, stirring constantly, for 2 minutes. Gradually whisk in the cream and milk and bring to simmering point. Add the salt, the nutmeg, white pepper, thyme and garlic, reduce the heat to low and simmer for 5 minutes. Remove the thyme sprigs.

3 Make a layer of half the potatoes in the prepared dish and season generously with salt and pepper. Top with half the sauce and cover with half the cheese. Repeat the layers with the remaining potatoes, sauce and cheese.

4 Bake in the preheated oven for about 1 hour, or until the top is browned and the potatoes are tender. Remove from the oven and leave to rest for 15 minutes before serving.

mini yorkshire puddings

ingredients
makes 6 puddings

30 g/1 oz beef dripping or 2 tbsp
    sunflower oil
140 g/5 oz plain flour
½ tsp salt
2 eggs
225 ml/8 fl oz milk

method

1 Grease six metal pudding moulds with the dripping,
then divide the remaining dripping between the
moulds. Preheat the oven to 220°C/425°F/Gas Mark 7,
placing the moulds in the oven so the dripping can
melt while the oven heats.

2 Sift the flour and salt together into a large mixing bowl
and make a well in the centre. Break the eggs into the
well, add the milk and beat, gradually drawing in the
flour from the side to make a smooth batter. Remove
the moulds from the oven and spoon in the batter until
they are about half full.

3 Bake in the preheated oven for 30–35 minutes, without
opening the door, until the puddings are well risen,
puffed and golden brown. Serve immediately, as they
will collapse if left to stand.

hush puppies

ingredients

makes 30–35

280 g/10 oz quick-cook polenta
70 g/2½ oz plain flour, sifted
1 small onion, finely chopped
1 tbsp caster sugar
2 tsp baking powder
½ tsp salt
175 ml/6 fl oz milk
1 egg, beaten
corn oil, for deep-frying

method

1 Stir the polenta, flour, onion, sugar, baking powder and salt together in a bowl and make a well in the centre.

2 Beat the milk and egg together in a jug, then pour into the dry ingredients and stir until a thick batter forms.

3 Heat at least 5 cm/2 inches of oil in a deep frying pan or saucepan over a high heat, until the temperature reaches 180°C/350°F, or until a cube of bread browns in 30 seconds.

4 Drop in as many teaspoonfuls of the batter as will fit without overcrowding the frying pan and cook, stirring constantly, until the hush puppies puff up and turn golden.

5 Remove from the oil with a slotted spoon and drain on kitchen paper. Reheat the oil, if necessary, and cook the remaining batter. Serve hot.

gravy

ingredients

*makes about 1.2 litres/
2 pints*

900 g/2 lb meat bones,
     raw or cooked
1 large onion, chopped
1 large carrot, chopped
2 celery sticks, chopped
1 bouquet garni
1.7 litres/3 pints water

method

1 Preheat the oven to 200°C/400°F/Gas Mark 6. Put the
   bones in a roasting tin and roast in the preheated oven
   for 20 minutes, or until browned. Remove from the
   oven and leave to cool.

2 Chop the bones into small pieces and put in a large
   saucepan with all the remaining ingredients. Bring to
   the boil, then reduce the heat, cover and simmer for
   2 hours.

3 Strain and leave until cold, then remove all traces of fat.
   Store, covered, in the refrigerator for up to 4 days. Boil
   vigorously for 5 minutes before using. The gravy can be
   frozen in ice-cube trays for up to 1 month.

red wine sauce

ingredients

makes 225 ml/8 fl oz

150 ml/5 fl oz gravy
   (see page 110)
4 tbsp red wine, such as a
   burgundy
1 tbsp redcurrant jelly

method

1 Blend the gravy with the wine and pour into a small,
   heavy-based saucepan. Add the redcurrant jelly and
   warm over a gentle heat, stirring, until blended.

2 Bring to the boil, then reduce the heat and simmer
   for 2 minutes. Serve hot.

coleslaw

ingredients
serves 10–12

150 ml/5 fl oz mayonnaise
150 ml/5 fl oz natural yogurt
dash of hot pepper sauce
1 head of white cabbage
4 carrots
1 green pepper, halved and
    deseeded
salt and pepper

method

1 Mix the mayonnaise, yogurt, hot pepper sauce, and salt and pepper to taste together in a small bowl. Chill in the refrigerator until required.

2 Cut the cabbage in half and then into quarters. Remove and discard the tough centre stalk. Finely shred the cabbage leaves. Wash the leaves under cold running water and dry thoroughly on kitchen paper. Roughly grate the carrots or shred in a food processor or on a mandoline. Finely chop the green pepper.

3 Mix the vegetables together in a large serving bowl and toss to mix. Pour over the dressing and toss until the vegetables are well coated. Cover and chill in the refrigerator until required.

corn relish

ingredients

makes about 600 g/
1 lb 5 oz

5 corn cobs, about 900 g/
    2 lb, husked
1 red pepper, deseeded and
    finely diced
2 celery sticks, very finely chopped
1 red onion, finely chopped
125 g/4½ oz sugar
1 tbsp salt
2 tbsp mustard powder
½ tsp celery seeds
small pinch of turmeric (optional)
225 ml/8 fl oz cider vinegar
125 ml/4 fl oz water

method

1 Bring a large saucepan of lightly salted water to the
boil and fill a bowl with iced water. Add the corn to
the boiling water, return the water to the boil and boil
for 2 minutes, or until the kernels are tender-crisp.
Using tongs, immediately plunge the cobs into the
cold water to halt cooking. Remove from the water
and cut the kernels from the cobs, then set aside.

2 Add the red pepper, celery and onion to the corn
cooking water, bring back to the boil and boil for
2 minutes, or until tender-crisp. Drain well and
return to the pan with the corn kernels.

3 Put the sugar, salt, mustard, celery seeds and turmeric,
if using, into a bowl and mix together, then stir in the
vinegar and water. Add to the pan, bring the liquid
to the boil, then reduce the heat and simmer for
15 minutes, stirring occasionally.

4 Ladle the relish into hot, sterilized preserving jars, filling
them to within 1 cm/½ inch of the top of each jar. Wipe
the rims and secure the lids. Leave the relish to cool
completely, then refrigerate for up to 2 months.

spicy tomato sauce

ingredients

serves 4

325 g/11½ oz passata
2 tbsp chopped fresh coriander
1 tbsp soy sauce
½ tsp chilli powder
2 tsp muscovado sugar
2 tsp mild mustard
5 tbsp vegetable stock

method

1 Combine all the ingredients in a small saucepan and bring to the boil. Reduce the heat to low, cover and simmer for 15 minutes.

2 Pour the mixture into a food processor or blender and blend well. Sieve thoroughly to remove any seeds.

3 Cool and serve immediately or store in the refrigerator until required.

classic strawberry jam

ingredients

makes about 1.5 kg/
3 lb 5 oz

1.5 kg/3 lb 5 oz ripe, unblemished
   whole strawberries, hulled
   and rinsed
2 freshly squeezed lemons, juice
   strained
1.5 kg/3 lb 5 oz preserving sugar
1 tsp butter

method

1 Place the strawberries in a preserving pan with the
   lemon juice, then simmer over a gentle heat for
   15–20 minutes, stirring occasionally, until the fruit
   has collapsed and is very soft.

2 Add the sugar and heat, stirring occasionally, until the
   sugar has completely dissolved. Add the butter, then
   bring to the boil and boil rapidly for 10–20 minutes, or
   until the jam has reached its setting point.

3 Leave to cool for 8–10 minutes, then skim and pot into
   warmed sterilized jars and immediately cover the tops
   with waxed discs. When completely cold, cover with
   cellophane or lids, label and store in a cool place.

orange & squash marmalade

ingredients

makes about 2.25 kg/5 lb

900 g/2 lb acorn squash or
    butternut squash (peeled and
    deseeded weight), cut into
    small chunks
6 blood oranges, scrubbed
150 ml/5 fl oz freshly squeezed
    lemon juice
small piece fresh ginger, peeled
    and grated
2 serrano chillies, deseeded and
    finely sliced
1.2 litres/2 pints water
1.25 kg/2 lb 12 oz preserving sugar

method

1 Place the squash in a large saucepan with a tight-fitting lid. Thinly slice two of the oranges without peeling, reserving the pips, and add to the saucepan.

2 Peel the remaining oranges, chop the flesh and add to the pan together with the lemon juice, grated ginger and sliced chillies. Tie up the orange pips in a piece of muslin and add to the pan with the water.

3 Bring to the boil, then reduce the heat, cover and simmer gently for 1 hour, or until the squash and oranges are very soft. If preferred, transfer the mixture to a preserving pan.

4 Add the sugar and heat gently, stirring, until the sugar has completely dissolved. Bring to the boil and boil rapidly for 15 minutes, or until the setting point is reached.

5 Skim, if necessary, then leave to cool for 10 minutes. Pot into warmed sterilized jars and immediately cover the tops with waxed discs. When completely cold, cover with cellophane or lids, label and store in a cool place.

cherry with brandy jam

ingredients

makes about 2.25 kg/5 lb

1.8 kg/4 lb dark cherries, such as morello, rinsed and stoned

125 ml/4 fl oz freshly squeezed lemon juice or 1½ tsp citric or tartaric acid

150 ml/5 fl oz water (optional)

1.25 kg/2 lb 12 oz granulated sugar

1 tsp butter

4 tbsp brandy

225 ml/8 fl oz liquid pectin

method

1 Roughly chop the cherries and place in a large preserving pan with the lemon juice. If using citric or tartaric acid, add to the pan with the water. Place the pan over a gentle heat, cover and simmer gently for 20 minutes, or until the cherries have collapsed and are very soft.

2 Add the sugar and heat, stirring frequently, until the sugar has completely dissolved. Add the butter and brandy, bring to the boil and boil rapidly for 3 minutes. Remove from the heat and stir in the pectin.

3 Leave to cool for 10 minutes then pot into warmed sterilized jars and cover the tops with waxed discs. When completely cold, cover with cellophane or lids, label and store in a cool place.

variation

Other spirits or liqueurs can be used in place of the brandy. Try kirsch, an orange-flavoured liqueur or a whisky liqueur.

just desserts

apple pie

ingredients

serves 6
pastry
350 g/12 oz plain flour
pinch of salt
85 g/3 oz butter or margarine,
    cut into small pieces
85 g/3 oz lard or white vegetable
    fat, cut into small pieces
about 6 tbsp cold water
beaten egg or milk, for glazing

filling
750 g–1 kg/1 lb 10 oz–2 lb 4 oz
    cooking apples, peeled, cored
    and sliced
125 g/4½ oz soft light brown sugar
    or caster sugar, plus extra for
    sprinkling
½–1 tsp ground cinnamon, mixed
    spice or ground ginger
1–2 tbsp water (optional)

method

1 To make the pastry, sift the flour and salt into a mixing bowl. Add the butter and lard and rub in with your fingertips until the mixture resembles fine breadcrumbs. Add the water and gather the mixture together into a dough. Wrap the dough and chill in the refrigerator for 30 minutes.

2 Preheat the oven to 220°C/425°F/Gas Mark 7. Roll out almost two thirds of the pastry thinly and use to line a deep 23-cm/9-inch pie plate or pie tin.

3 To make the filling, mix the apples with the sugar and spice and pack into the pastry case. Add the water if needed, particularly if the apples are not very juicy.

4 Roll out the remaining pastry to form a lid. Dampen the edges of the pie rim with water and position the lid, pressing the edges firmly together. Trim and crimp the edges.

5 Using the trimmings, cut out leaves or other shapes to decorate the top of the pie. Dampen and attach. Glaze the top of the pie with the beaten egg and make one or two slits in the top.

6 Place the pie on a baking tray and bake in the preheated oven for 20 minutes, then reduce the oven temperature to 180°C/350°F/Gas Mark 4 and bake for a further 30 minutes, or until the pastry is a light golden brown. Serve hot or cold, sprinkled with sugar.

bread & butter pudding

ingredients

serves 4–6

85 g/3 oz butter, softened
6 thick slices of white bread
55 g/2 oz mixed dried fruit, such as
    sultanas, currants and raisins
25 g/1 oz mixed peel
3 large eggs
300 ml/10 fl oz milk
150 ml/5 fl oz double cream
55 g/2 oz caster sugar
whole nutmeg, for grating
1 tbsp demerara sugar
pouring cream, to serve (optional)

method

1 Preheat the oven to 180°C/350°F/Gas Mark 4.

2 Use a little of the butter to grease a 20 x 25-cm/
  8 x 10-inch baking dish. Butter the slices of bread,
  cut into quarters and arrange half of the slices
  overlapping in the prepared baking dish.

3 Scatter half the fruit and mixed peel over the bread,
  cover with the remaining bread slices, then add the
  remaining fruit and mixed peel.

4 In a mixing jug, whisk the eggs well and mix in the
  milk, cream and sugar. Pour over the pudding and
  leave to stand for 15 minutes to allow the bread to
  soak up some of the egg mixture. Tuck in most of the
  fruit as you don't want it to burn in the oven.

5 Grate nutmeg to taste over the top of the pudding,
  then sprinkle over the demerara sugar.

6 Place the pudding on a baking tray and bake at the top
  of the preheated oven for 30–40 minutes, until just set
  and golden brown.

7 Remove from the oven and serve warm with a little
  cream, if using.

banana cream pie

ingredients

serves 8–10

flour, for dusting

350 g/12 oz ready-made
    shortcrust pastry, thawed,
    if frozen

4 large egg yolks

85 g/3 oz caster sugar

4 tbsp cornflour

pinch of salt

450 ml/16 fl oz milk

1 tsp vanilla extract

3 bananas

½ tbsp lemon juice

350 ml/12 fl oz double cream,
    whipped with 3 tbsp icing
    sugar, to decorate

method

1 Preheat the oven to 200°C/400°F/Gas Mark 6. Very lightly flour a rolling pin and use to roll out the pastry on a lightly floured work surface into a 30-cm/12-inch round. Line a 23-cm/9-inch pie plate with the pastry, then trim the excess pastry and prick the base all over with a fork. Line the pastry case with greaseproof paper and fill with baking beans.

2 Bake in the preheated oven for 15 minutes, or until the pastry is a light golden colour. Remove the paper and beans and prick the base again. Return to the oven and bake for a further 5–10 minutes, until golden and dry. Leave to cool completely on a wire rack.

3 Meanwhile, put the egg yolks, sugar, cornflour and salt into a bowl and beat until blended and pale in colour. Beat in the milk and vanilla extract.

4 Pour the mixture into a heavy-based saucepan over a medium–high heat and bring to the boil, stirring, until smooth and thick. Reduce the heat to low and simmer, stirring, for 2 minutes. Strain the mixture into a bowl and set aside to cool.

5 Slice the bananas, place in a bowl with the lemon juice and toss. Arrange them in the cooled pastry case, then top with the custard and chill in the refrigerator for at least 2 hours. Spread the cream over the top of the pie and serve immediately.

lemon meringue pie

ingredients

serves 6–8

pastry

150 g/5½ oz plain flour, plus extra
    for dusting
85 g/3 oz butter, cut into small
    pieces, plus extra for greasing
35 g/1¼ oz icing sugar, sifted
finely grated rind of ½ lemon
½ egg yolk, beaten
1½ tbsp milk

filling

3 tbsp cornflour
300 ml/10 fl oz water
juice and grated rind of 2 lemons
175 g/6 oz caster sugar
2 eggs, separated

method

1 To make the pastry, sift the flour into a bowl. Rub in the butter with your fingertips until the mixture resembles fine breadcrumbs. Mix in the remaining ingredients. Turn out onto a lightly floured work surface and knead briefly. Wrap in clingfilm and chill in the refrigerator for 30 minutes.

2 Preheat the oven to 180°C/350°F/Gas Mark 4. Grease a 20-cm/8-inch round tart tin. Roll out the pastry to a thickness of 5 mm/¼ inch, then use it to line the base and side of the tin. Prick all over with a fork, line with baking paper and fill with baking beans. Bake in the preheated oven for 15 minutes. Remove the pastry case from the oven and take out the paper and beans. Reduce the oven temperature to 150°C/300°F/Gas Mark 2.

3 To make the filling, mix the cornflour with a little of the water to form a paste. Put the remaining water in a saucepan. Stir in the lemon juice, lemon rind and cornflour paste. Bring to the boil, stirring, and cook for 2 minutes. Leave to cool slightly. Stir in 5 tablespoons of the caster sugar and the egg yolks, then pour into the pastry case.

4 Whisk the egg whites in a clean, grease-free bowl until stiff. Gradually whisk in the remaining caster sugar and spread over the pie. Bake for a further 40 minutes. Remove from the oven, cool and serve.

lime pie

ingredients

serves 8
crumb crust
175 g/6 oz digestive or ginger
biscuits
2 tbsp caster sugar
½ tsp ground cinnamon
70 g/2½ oz butter, melted, plus
extra for greasing

filling
400 ml/14 fl oz canned condensed
milk
125 ml/4 fl oz freshly squeezed
lime juice
finely grated rind of 3 limes
4 egg yolks
whipped cream, to serve

method

1 Preheat the oven to 160°C/325°F/Gas Mark 3. Lightly grease a 23-cm/9-inch round tart tin, about 4 cm/1½ inches deep.

2 To make the crumb crust, put the biscuits, sugar and cinnamon in a food processor and process until fine crumbs form – do not overprocess to a powder. Add the melted butter and process again until moistened.

3 Tip the crumb mixture into the prepared tart tin and press over the base and up the side. Place the tart tin on a baking tray and bake in the preheated oven for 5 minutes.

4 Meanwhile, to make the filling, beat the condensed milk, lime juice, lime rind and egg yolks together in a bowl until well blended.

5 Remove the tart tin from the oven, pour the filling into the crumb crust and spread out to the edges. Return to the oven for a further 15 minutes, or until the filling is set around the edges but still wobbly in the centre.

6 Leave to cool completely on a wire rack, then cover and chill for at least 2 hours. Spread thickly with whipped cream and serve.

rhubarb crumble

ingredients

serves 6

900 g/2 lb rhubarb
115 g/4 oz caster sugar
grated rind and juice of 1 orange
home-made vanilla custard
    (see page 164), to serve

crumble

225 g/8 oz plain flour or
    wholemeal flour
115 g/4 oz butter
115 g/4 oz soft light brown sugar
1 tsp ground ginger

method

1 Preheat the oven to 190°C/375°F/Gas Mark 5.

2 Cut the rhubarb into 2.5-cm/1-inch lengths and place
    in a 1.7-litre/3-pint ovenproof dish with the sugar and
    the orange rind and juice.

3 To make the crumble, place the flour in a mixing bowl
    and rub in the butter until the mixture resembles
    coarse breadcrumbs. Stir in the sugar and the ginger.

4 Spread the crumble evenly over the fruit and press
    down lightly using a fork.

5 Place on a baking tray and bake in the centre of the
    preheated oven for 25–30 minutes, until the crumble
    is golden brown. Serve warm with home-made
    vanilla custard.

baked rice pudding

ingredients
serves 4–6

1 tbsp melted unsalted butter
115 g/4 oz pudding rice
55 g/2 oz caster sugar
850 ml/1½ pints milk
½ tsp vanilla extract
40 g/1½ oz unsalted butter,
    chilled and cut into pieces
whole nutmeg, for grating
cream, jam, fresh fruit purée,
    stewed fruit, honey or ice
    cream, to serve (optional)

method

1 Preheat the oven to 150°C/300°F/Gas Mark 2. Grease a 1.2-litre/2-pint baking dish (a gratin dish is good) with the melted butter, place the rice in the dish and sprinkle with the sugar.

2 Heat the milk in a saucepan until almost boiling, then pour over the rice. Add the vanilla extract and stir well to dissolve the sugar.

3 Cut the butter into small pieces and scatter over the surface of the pudding.

4 Grate nutmeg to taste over the top. Place the dish on a baking tray and bake in the centre of the preheated oven for 1½–2 hours until the pudding is well browned on the top. Stir after the first 30 minutes of cooking to disperse the rice. Serve hot, topped with cream, if using.

new york cheesecake

ingredients

serves 10

100 g/3½ oz butter, plus extra for
    greasing
150 g/5½ oz digestive biscuits,
    finely crushed
1 tbsp granulated sugar
900 g/2 lb cream cheese
250 g/9 oz caster sugar
2 tbsp plain flour
1 tsp vanilla extract
finely grated zest of 1 orange
finely grated zest of 1 lemon
3 eggs
2 egg yolks
300 ml/10 fl oz double cream

method

1 Preheat the oven to 180°C/350°F/Gas Mark 4. Place a
  small saucepan over a low flame, add the butter and
  heat until it melts. Remove from the heat, stir in the
  biscuits and granulated sugar and mix through.

2 Press the biscuit mixture tightly into the base of a
  23-cm/9-inch springform cake tin. Place in the
  preheated oven and bake for 10 minutes. Remove
  from the oven and leave to cool on a wire rack.

3 Increase the oven temperature to 200°C/400°F/
  Gas Mark 6. Use an electric mixer to beat the cheese
  until creamy, then gradually add the caster sugar and
  flour and beat until smooth. Increase the speed and
  beat in the vanilla extract, orange zest and lemon zest,
  then beat in the eggs and egg yolks one at a time.
  Finally, beat in the cream.

4 Grease the side of the cake tin and pour in the
  filling. Smooth the top, transfer to the oven and bake
  for 15 minutes, then reduce the temperature to
  110°C/225°F/Gas Mark ¼ and bake for a further
  30 minutes. Turn off the oven and leave the
  cheesecake in it for 2 hours to cool and set. Cover
  and chill in the refrigerator overnight.

5 Slide a knife around the edge of the cake then unfasten
  the tin, cut the cheesecake into slices and serve.

sticky toffee pudding

ingredients

serves 4

pudding
75 g/2¾ oz sultanas
150 g/5½ oz stoned dates, chopped
1 tsp bicarbonate of soda
2 tbsp butter, plus extra for greasing
200 g/7 oz soft light brown sugar
2 eggs
200 g/7 oz self-raising flour, sifted

sticky toffee sauce
2 tbsp butter
175 ml/6 fl oz double cream
200 g/7 oz soft light brown sugar
zested rind of 1 orange, to decorate
freshly whipped cream, to serve (optional)

method

1 To make the pudding, put the sultanas, dates and bicarbonate of soda into a heatproof bowl. Cover with boiling water and leave to soak.

2 Preheat the oven to 180°C/350°F/Gas Mark 4. Grease a round cake tin, 20 cm/8 inches in diameter.

3 Put the butter in a separate bowl, add the sugar and mix well. Beat in the eggs then fold in the flour. Drain the soaked fruit, add to the bowl and mix. Spoon the mixture evenly into the prepared cake tin.

4 Transfer to the preheated oven and bake for 35–40 minutes. The pudding is cooked when a skewer inserted into the centre comes out clean.

5 About 5 minutes before the end of the cooking time, make the sauce. Melt the butter in a saucepan over a medium heat. Stir in the cream and sugar and bring to the boil, stirring constantly. Reduce the heat and simmer for 5 minutes.

6 Turn out the pudding onto a serving plate and pour over the sauce. Decorate with zested orange rind and serve with whipped cream, if using.

chocolate pudding

ingredients

serves 4–6

100 g/3½ oz sugar
4 tbsp cocoa powder
2 tbsp cornflour
pinch of salt
350 ml/12 fl oz milk
1 egg, beaten
55 g/2 oz butter
½ tsp vanilla extract
double cream, to serve

method

1 Put the sugar, cocoa powder, cornflour and salt into a heatproof bowl, stir and set aside.

2 Pour the milk into a saucepan and heat over a medium heat until just simmering. Do not bring to the boil.

3 Keeping the pan over a medium heat, spoon a little of the simmering milk into the sugar mixture and blend, then stir this mixture into the milk in the pan. Beat in the egg and half the butter and reduce the heat to low.

4 Simmer for 5–8 minutes, stirring frequently, until the mixture thickens. Remove from the heat and add the vanilla extract and the remaining butter, stirring until the butter melts and is absorbed.

5 The pudding can be served hot or chilled, with cream for pouring over. If chilling the pudding, spoon it into a serving bowl and leave to cool completely, then press clingfilm onto the surface to prevent a skin forming and chill in the refrigerator until required.

pecan pie

ingredients

serves 8

pastry

200 g/7 oz plain flour, plus extra
for dusting
115 g/4 oz unsalted butter, cut into
small pieces
2 tbsp caster sugar
a little cold water

filling

70 g/2½ oz unsalted butter
100 g/3½ oz light muscovado
sugar
140 g/5 oz golden syrup
2 large eggs, beaten
1 tsp vanilla extract
115 g/4 oz pecan nuts

method

1 To make the pastry, place the flour in a bowl and rub in
the butter with your fingertips until it resembles fine
breadcrumbs. Stir in the sugar and add enough cold
water to mix to a firm dough. Wrap in clingfilm and chill
for 15 minutes, until firm enough to roll out.

2 Preheat the oven to 200°C/400°F/Gas Mark 6. Roll out
the pastry on a lightly floured surface and use to line a
23-cm/9-inch loose-based round tart tin. Prick the base
with a fork. Chill for 15 minutes.

3 Place the tart tin on a baking tray and line with a sheet
of baking paper and baking beans. Bake blind in the
preheated oven for 10 minutes. Remove the baking
beans and paper and bake for a further 5 minutes.
Reduce the oven temperature to 180°C/350°F/
Gas Mark 4.

4 To make the filling, place the butter, sugar and golden
syrup in a saucepan and heat gently until melted.
Remove from the heat and quickly beat in the eggs
and vanilla extract.

5 Roughly chop the nuts and stir into the mixture. Pour
into the pastry case and bake for 35–40 minutes, until
the filling is just set. Serve warm or cold.

pumpkin pie

ingredients

serves 6

1.8 kg/4 lb sweet pumpkin, halved and deseeded, stem and stringy bits removed

140 g/5 oz plain flour, plus extra for dusting

¼ tsp baking powder

1½ tsp ground cinnamon

¾ tsp ground nutmeg

¾ tsp ground cloves

1 tsp salt

50 g/1¾ oz caster sugar

55 g/2 oz cold unsalted butter, diced, plus extra for greasing

3 eggs

400 ml/14 fl oz canned condensed milk

½ tsp vanilla extract

1 tbsp demerara sugar

streusel topping

2 tbsp plain flour

4 tbsp demerara sugar

1 tsp ground cinnamon

2 tbsp cold unsalted butter, diced

75 g/2¾ oz pecan nuts, chopped

75 g/2¾ oz walnuts, chopped

method

1 Preheat the oven to 190°C/375°F/Gas Mark 5. Bake the pumpkin halves, face down in a shallow tin, covered with foil, for 1½ hours. When cool, puree the flesh in a food processor. Drain off any liquid, cover and chill.

2 Grease a 23-cm/9-inch round tart tin. Sift the flour and baking powder into a bowl. Stir in ½ tsp of the cinnamon, ¼ tsp of the nutmeg, ¼ tsp of the cloves, ½ tsp of the salt and all the caster sugar. Rub in the butter until the mixture resembles fine breadcrumbs, then make a well in the centre. Lightly beat 1 of the eggs and pour it into the well. Mix together, then shape into a ball. Roll out the dough on a lightly floured work surface and line the tin. Trim the edges, cover and chill for 30 minutes.

3 Preheat the oven to 220°C/425°F/Gas Mark 7. Put the pumpkin purée in a large bowl, then stir in the condensed milk, the remaining eggs, spices, salt, vanilla extract and demerara sugar. Pour into the pastry case and bake in the preheated oven for 15 minutes.

4 For the streusel topping, mix the flour, sugar and cinnamon together in a bowl, rub in the butter, then stir in the nuts. Reduce the oven temperature to 180°C/350°F/Gas Mark 4. Sprinkle the topping over the pie then return to the oven and bake for a further 35 minutes. Serve warm.

latticed cherry pie

ingredients

serves 8

pastry

140 g/5 oz plain flour, plus extra
 for dusting
¼ tsp baking powder
½ tsp mixed spice
½ tsp salt
50 g/1¾ oz caster sugar
55 g/2 oz unsalted butter, chilled
 and diced, plus extra for
 greasing
1 egg, beaten, plus extra for
 glazing
water, for sealing

filling

900 g/2 lb stoned fresh cherries,
 or canned cherries, drained
150 g/5½ oz caster sugar
½ tsp almond extract
2 tsp cherry brandy
¼ tsp mixed spice
2 tbsp cornflour
2 tbsp water
25 g/1 oz unsalted butter, melted

method

1 To make the pastry, sift the flour with the baking
 powder into a large bowl. Stir in the mixed spice, salt
 and sugar. Rub in the butter until the mixture resembles
 fine breadcrumbs. Make a well in the centre, pour in the
 egg and mix into a dough. Cut the dough in half, wrap
 and chill for 30 minutes.

2 Preheat the oven to 220°C/425°F/Gas Mark 7. Grease a
 23-cm/9-inch round pie dish. Roll out the doughs into
 two rounds, each 30 cm/12 inches in diameter. Use one
 to line the pie dish.

3 To make the filling, put half the cherries and all the
 sugar in a saucepan. Bring to a simmer and stir in the
 almond extract, brandy and mixed spice. In a bowl, mix
 the cornflour and water into a paste. Stir the paste into
 the saucepan, then boil until the mixture thickens. Stir
 in the remaining cherries, pour into the pastry case,
 then drizzle with the melted butter.

4 Cut the remaining pastry into strips 1 cm/½ inch wide.
 Lay the strips over the filling, crossing to form a lattice.
 Trim and seal the edges with water. Use your fingers to
 crimp the rim, then glaze the top with the beaten egg.
 Cover with foil, then bake for 30 minutes in the
 preheated oven. Discard the foil, then bake for a further
 15 minutes, or until golden. Serve warm.

baked spicy pudding

ingredients

serves 4–6

2 tbsp raisins or sultanas
5 tbsp quick-cook polenta
350 ml/12 fl oz milk
4 tbsp treacle
2 tbsp soft dark brown sugar
1/2 tsp salt
30 g/1 oz butter, diced, plus extra for greasing
2 tsp ground ginger
1/4 tsp cinnamon
1/4 tsp ground nutmeg
2 eggs, beaten
vanilla ice cream or maple syrup, to serve

method

1 Preheat the oven to 150°C/300°F/Gas Mark 2. Generously grease a 850-ml/1½-pint ovenproof serving dish and set aside. Put the raisins in a sieve with 1 tablespoon of the polenta and toss well together. Shake off the excess polenta and set aside.

2 Put the milk and treacle into a saucepan over a medium–high heat and stir until the treacle is dissolved. Add the sugar and salt and continue stirring until the sugar is dissolved. Sprinkle over the remaining polenta and bring to the boil, stirring constantly. Reduce the heat and simmer for 3–5 minutes, until the mixture is thickened.

3 Remove the pan from the heat, add the butter, ginger, cinnamon and nutmeg and stir until the butter is melted. Add the eggs and beat until they are incorporated, then stir in the raisins. Pour the mixture into the prepared dish.

4 Put the dish in a small roasting tin and pour in enough boiling water to come halfway up the side of the dish. Put the dish in the preheated oven and bake, uncovered, for 1¾–2 hours, until the pudding is set and a wooden skewer inserted in the centre comes out clean.

5 Serve immediately, straight from the dish, with a dollop of ice cream on top.

apple turnovers

ingredients

makes 8 turnovers

250 g/9 oz ready-made puff
    pastry, thawed, if frozen
flour, for dusting
milk, for glazing

filling

450 g/1 lb cooking apples, peeled,
    cored and chopped
grated rind of 1 lemon (optional)
pinch of ground cloves (optional)
3 tbsp sugar

orange sugar

1 tbsp sugar, for sprinkling
finely grated rind of 1 orange

orange cream

250 ml/9 fl oz double cream
grated rind of 1 orange and juice of
    ¹/₂ orange
icing sugar, to taste

method

1 To make the filling, mix together the apples, lemon rind
and ground cloves, if using, but do not add the sugar.
For the orange sugar, mix together the sugar and
orange rind.

2 Preheat the oven to 220°C/425°F/Gas Mark 7. Roll
out the pastry on a floured work surface into a
60 x 30-cm/24 x 12-inch rectangle. Cut the pastry in
half lengthways, then across into four to make eight
15-cm/6-inch squares.

3 Mix the sugar into the apple filling. Brush each square
lightly with milk and place a little of the apple filling in
the centre. Fold over one corner diagonally to meet the
opposite one, making a triangular turnover, and press
the edges together very firmly. Place on a non-stick
baking sheet. Repeat with the remaining squares.

4 Brush the turnovers with milk and sprinkle with a little
of the orange sugar. Bake for 15–20 minutes, until
puffed and well browned. Cool the turnovers on a
wire rack.

5 For the orange cream, whip the cream, orange rind and
orange juice together until thick. Add a little sugar to
taste and whip again. Serve the turnovers warm, with
dollops of orange cream.

apple fritters

ingredients

makes 12 fritters

300 g/10½ oz eating apples, such
    as Granny Smith, peeled, cored
    and diced
1 tsp lemon juice
2 eggs, separated
sunflower oil, for deep-frying
    and greasing
150 ml/5 fl oz milk
15 g/½ oz butter, melted
70 g/2½ oz plain white flour
70 g/2½ oz plain wholemeal flour
2 tbsp sugar
¼ tsp salt

cinnamon glaze

55 g/2 oz icing sugar
½ tsp ground cinnamon
1 tbsp milk, plus extra, if needed

method

1 To make the cinnamon glaze, sift the sugar and
   cinnamon into a small bowl. Slowly stir in the milk until
   smooth, then set aside.

2 Put the apples in a small bowl, add the lemon juice,
   toss and set aside. Beat the egg whites in a separate
   bowl until stiff peaks form, then set aside.

3 Heat enough oil for deep-frying in a deep-fat fryer or
   heavy-based saucepan until it reaches 180°C/350°F, or
   until a cube of bread browns in 30 seconds.

4 Put the egg yolks and milk into a large bowl and beat
   together, then stir in the butter. Sift in both the flours,
   the sugar and salt, then stir the dry ingredients into the
   wet ingredients until just combined. Stir in the apples
   and their juices, then fold in the egg whites.

5 Lightly grease a spoon and use it to drop batter into
   the hot oil, without overcrowding the pan. Fry the
   fritters for 2–3 minutes, turning once, until golden
   brown on both sides. Drain on kitchen paper, then
   transfer to a wire rack. Repeat until all the batter is used.

6 Stir the glaze and add a little extra milk, if necessary.
   Drizzle the glaze over the fritters and leave to stand for
   3–5 minutes to firm up. Serve immediately.

banana splits

ingredients

serves 4

4 bananas
6 tbsp chopped mixed nuts,
    to serve

vanilla ice cream

300 ml/10 fl oz milk
1 tsp vanilla extract
3 egg yolks
100 g/3½ oz caster sugar
300 ml/10 fl oz double cream,
    whipped

chocolate rum sauce

125 g/4½ oz plain chocolate,
    broken into small pieces
2½ tbsp butter
6 tbsp water
1 tbsp rum

method

1 To make the vanilla ice cream, heat the milk and vanilla extract in a saucepan over a medium heat until almost boiling. Beat the egg yolks and sugar together in a bowl. Remove the milk from the heat and stir a little into the egg mixture. Transfer the mixture to the pan and stir over a low heat until thickened. Do not allow to boil. Remove from the heat.

2 Leave to cool for about 30 minutes, fold in the cream, cover with clingfilm and chill in the refrigerator for 1 hour. Transfer to an ice-cream maker and process for 15 minutes.

3 Alternatively, transfer into a freezerproof container and freeze for 1 hour, then place in a bowl and beat to break up the ice crystals. Return to the container and freeze for 30 minutes. Repeat twice more, freezing for 30 minutes and whisking each time.

4 To make the chocolate rum sauce, melt the chocolate and butter with the water in a saucepan, stirring constantly. Remove from the heat and stir in the rum. Peel the bananas, slice lengthways and arrange on four serving dishes. Top with ice cream and nuts and serve with the sauce.

chocolate fudge

ingredients

makes 32 pieces

2 tbsp cocoa powder

300 ml/10 fl oz milk

125 g/4½ oz plain chocolate, at least 85 per cent cocoa solids, finely chopped

800 g/1 lb 12 oz caster sugar

125 g/4½ oz butter, chopped, plus extra for greasing

pinch of salt

1½ tsp vanilla extract

175 g/6 oz pecan nuts, walnuts or toasted hazelnuts, or a mixture of nuts, chopped

method

1 Line a 20-cm/8-inch square cake tin with greased foil.

2 Put the cocoa powder into a small bowl, add 2 tablespoons of the milk and stir until blended. Pour the remaining milk into a large, heavy-based saucepan, then add the cocoa mixture and chocolate and simmer over a medium–high heat, stirring, until the chocolate melts. Add the sugar, butter and salt, reduce the heat to low and stir until the butter is melted, the sugar is dissolved and you can't feel any of the grains when you rub a spoon against the side of the pan.

3 Increase the heat and bring the mixture to the boil. Cover the pan and boil for 2 minutes, then uncover and continue boiling, without stirring, until the temperature reaches 115°C/239°F, or until a small amount of the mixture forms a soft ball when dropped in cold water.

4 Remove the pan from the heat, stir in the vanilla extract and beat the fudge until it thickens. Stir in the nuts. Pour the fudge mixture into the prepared tin and use a wet spatula to smooth the surface. Set aside and leave to stand for at least 2 hours to become firm. Lift the fudge out of the tin, then peel off the foil and cut into squares. Store the fudge for up to one week in an airtight container.

home-made vanilla custard

ingredients

serves 4–6

300 ml/10 fl oz milk
2 eggs
2 tsp caster sugar
1 vanilla pod, split, or 1 tsp vanilla
    extract

method

1 Put 2 tablespoons of the milk, the eggs and sugar into a heatproof bowl that will fit over a saucepan of simmering water without the bottom of the bowl touching the water, then set aside.

2 Heat the remaining milk just until small bubbles appear around the edge. Scrape half the vanilla seeds into the milk and add the pod. Remove the pan from the heat, cover and leave to infuse for 30 minutes.

3 Bring a kettle of water to the boil. Meanwhile, using an electric mixer, beat the milk, eggs and sugar until pale and thick. Slowly beat in the warm milk.

4 Pour a thin layer of boiling water into a saucepan, place over a low heat and fit the bowl containing the milk mixture on top. Cook, stirring constantly, for 10–15 minutes, until the sauce thickens. It is important that the bottom of the bowl never touches the water and that the sauce doesn't boil.

5 Strain the hot custard into a jug. Stir in the vanilla extract (if using). The custard can be used immediately, or cooled and chilled for up to one day. The sauce will thicken on cooling.

chocolate brandy sauce

ingredients

serves 4

250 g/9 oz plain chocolate
    (must contain at least
    50 per cent cocoa solids)
100 ml/3½ fl oz double cream
2 tbsp brandy

method

1 Break or chop the chocolate into small pieces and place in the top of a double boiler or in a heatproof bowl set over a saucepan of simmering water.

2 Pour in the cream and stir until melted and smooth. Stir in the brandy, pour into a jug and serve.

white chocolate fudge sauce

ingredients

serves 4

150 ml/5 fl oz double cream
4 tbsp unsalted butter,
    cut into small pieces
3 tbsp caster sugar
175 g/6 oz white chocolate,
    broken into pieces
2 tbsp brandy

method

1 Pour the cream into the top of a double boiler or a heatproof bowl set over a saucepan of gently simmering water. Add the butter and sugar and stir until the mixture is smooth. Remove from the heat.

2 Stir in the chocolate, a few pieces at a time, waiting until each batch has melted before adding the next. Add the brandy and stir the sauce until smooth. Cool to room temperature before serving.

variation

Give this sauce a citrus zing by replacing the brandy with the same quantity of an orange-flavoured liqueur.

baked delights

classic oatmeal cookies

ingredients

makes 30 cookies

175 g/6 oz butter, plus extra
    for greasing
275 g/9¾ oz demerara sugar
1 egg
4 tbsp water
1 tsp vanilla extract
375 g/13 oz rolled oats
140 g/5 oz plain flour
1 tsp salt
½ tsp bicarbonate of soda

method

1 Preheat the oven to 180°C/350°F/Gas Mark 4 and grease a large baking tray.

2 Cream the butter and sugar together in a large mixing bowl. Beat in the egg, water and vanilla extract until the mixture is smooth. In a separate bowl, mix the oats, flour, salt and bicarbonate of soda.

3 Gradually stir the oat mixture into the creamed mixture until thoroughly combined.

4 Place tablespoonfuls of the mixture onto the prepared baking tray, making sure they are well spaced. Transfer to the preheated oven and bake for 15 minutes, or until the biscuits are golden brown.

5 Using a palette knife, carefully transfer the cookies to wire racks to cool completely.

black & white cookies

ingredients

makes 20 cookies

115 g/4 oz unsalted butter, plus extra for greasing
1 tsp vanilla extract
175 g/6 oz caster sugar
2 eggs, beaten
300 g/10½ oz plain flour
½ tsp baking powder
200 ml/7 fl oz milk

icing

225 g/8 oz icing sugar
125 ml/4 fl oz double cream
⅛ tsp vanilla extract
75 g/2¾ oz plain chocolate, broken into pieces

method

1 Preheat the oven to 190°C/375°F/Gas Mark 5. Grease three baking sheets. Place the butter, vanilla extract and caster sugar in a large bowl. Beat the mixture with a whisk until light and fluffy and then beat in the eggs one at a time.

2 Sift the flour and baking powder and fold into the creamed mixture, loosening with milk as you go until both are used up and the mixture is of dropping consistency.

3 Drop heaped tablespoonfuls of the mixture, spaced well apart, on the prepared baking sheets. Place in the preheated oven and bake for 15 minutes until turning golden at the edges and light to the touch. Transfer to wire racks to cool completely.

4 To make the icing, put the icing sugar in a bowl and mix in half the cream and all the vanilla extract. The consistency should be thick but spreadable. Using a palette knife, spread half of each cookie with white icing. Now, melt the chocolate in a heatproof bowl over a pan of simmering water. The base of the bowl should not touch the water. Remove from the heat and stir in the remaining cream. Spread the dark icing over the uncoated cookie halves.

chocolate chip cookies

ingredients

makes 30 cookies

175 g/6 oz plain flour

1 tsp baking powder

125 g/4½ oz soft margarine, plus
    extra for greasing

85 g/3 oz light muscovado sugar

55 g/2 oz caster sugar

½ tsp vanilla extract

1 egg

125 g/4½ oz plain chocolate chips

method

1 Preheat the oven to 190°C/375°F/Gas Mark 5. Lightly grease two baking trays.

2 Place all of the ingredients in a large mixing bowl and beat until well combined.

3 Place tablespoonfuls of the mixture on the prepared baking trays, spacing them well apart to allow for spreading during cooking.

4 Bake in the preheated oven for 10–12 minutes, or until the cookies are golden brown. Using a palette knife, transfer the cookies to a wire rack to cool completely.

5 Serve immediately or store in an airtight container.

millionaires' shortbread

ingredients

makes 12 slices

115 g/4 oz butter, plus extra for greasing
175 g/6 oz plain flour
55 g/2 oz golden caster sugar
200 g/7 oz plain chocolate, broken into pieces

filling

175 g/6 oz butter
115 g/4 oz golden caster sugar
3 tbsp golden syrup
400 ml/14 fl oz canned condensed milk

method

1 Preheat the oven to 180°C/350°F/Gas Mark 4. Grease and line the base of a 23-cm/9-inch shallow, square cake tin.

2 Place the butter, flour and sugar in a food processor and process until the mixture begins to bind together. Press it into the prepared tin and smooth the top. Bake in the preheated oven for 20–25 minutes, or until golden.

3 Meanwhile, make the filling. Place the butter, sugar, golden syrup and condensed milk in a saucepan and heat gently over a low heat until the sugar is dissolved.

4 Bring to the boil and simmer for 6–8 minutes, stirring constantly, until the mixture becomes very thick. Pour over the shortbread base and leave to chill in the refrigerator until firm.

5 Place the chocolate in a heatproof bowl set over a saucepan of gently simmering water and stir until melted. Leave to cool slightly, then spread over the caramel. Chill in the refrigerator until set. Cut the shortbread into 12 pieces with a sharp knife and serve.

chocolate brownies

ingredients

makes 16 squares

groundnut oil, for greasing
225 g/8 oz plain chocolate, at least
    60 per cent cocoa solids
175 g/6 oz butter
3 large eggs
100 g/3½ oz caster sugar
175 g/6 oz self-raising flour
100 g/3½ oz walnuts or blanched
    hazelnuts, chopped
50 g/1¾ oz milk chocolate chips

method

1 Preheat the oven to 180°C/350°F/Gas Mark 4. Lightly grease a 25-cm/10-inch square non-stick, shallow baking tin.

2 Break the chocolate into a heatproof bowl and place over a small saucepan of simmering water. It is important that the base of the bowl doesn't touch the water.

3 Add the butter to the chocolate, set the bowl over the saucepan and heat the water to a slow simmer. Leave the chocolate, undisturbed, to melt very slowly – this will take about 10 minutes. Remove the bowl from the pan and stir well to combine the chocolate and the butter.

4 Meanwhile, beat the eggs and sugar together in a bowl until pale cream in colour. Stir in the melted chocolate mixture, then add the flour, nuts and chocolate chips. Mix everything together well.

5 Tip the mixture into the prepared baking tin and bake in the preheated oven for 30 minutes, or until the top is set – if the centre is still slightly sticky, that will be all the better. Leave to cool in the tin, then lift out and cut into squares.

raisin bran muffins

ingredients

makes 12 muffins

140 g/5 oz plain flour
1 tbsp baking powder
140 g/5 oz wheat bran
115 g/4 oz caster sugar
150 g/5½ oz raisins
2 eggs
250 ml/9 fl oz skimmed milk
90 ml/ 6 tbsp sunflower oil,
    plus extra for greasing
1 tsp vanilla extract

method

1 Preheat the oven to 200°C/400°F/Gas Mark 6. Grease a 12-cup muffin tin or line with 12 paper cases. Sift the flour and baking powder together into a large bowl. Stir in the bran, sugar and raisins.

2 Lightly beat the eggs in a large jug or bowl, then beat in the milk, oil and vanilla extract. Make a well in the centre of the dry ingredients and pour in the beaten liquid ingredients. Stir gently until just combined; do not over-mix.

3 Spoon the mixture into the prepared muffin tin. Bake in the preheated oven for about 20 minutes, until well risen, golden brown and firm to the touch.

4 Leave the muffins in the tin for 5 minutes then serve warm or transfer to a wire rack and leave to cool.

vanilla-frosted cupcakes

ingredients

makes 12 cupcakes

115 g/4 oz butter, softened
115 g/4 oz caster sugar
2 eggs, lightly beaten
115 g/4 oz self-raising flour
1 tbsp milk
1 tbsp coloured sprinkles

frosting

175 g/6 oz unsalted butter, softened
1 tsp vanilla extract
280 g/10 oz icing sugar, sifted

method

1 Preheat the oven to 180°C/350°F/Gas Mark 4. Put 12 paper baking cases in a bun tray or put 12 double-layer paper cases on a baking tray.

2 Put the butter and sugar in a bowl. Beat together until light and fluffy. Gradually beat in the eggs. Sift in the flour and fold in with the milk.

3 Spoon the mixture into the paper cases. Bake in the preheated oven for 20 minutes until golden brown and firm to the touch. Transfer to a wire rack to cool.

4 To make the frosting, put the butter and vanilla extract in a bowl and beat until pale and very soft. Gradually add the icing sugar, beating well after each addition.

5 Spoon the frosting into a large piping bag fitted with a medium star-shaped nozzle and pipe swirls of frosting on the top of each cupcake. Serve decorated with sprinkles.

traditional scones

ingredients

makes 10–12 scones

450 g/1 lb plain flour, plus
extra for dusting
½ tsp salt
2 tsp baking powder
55 g/2 oz butter
2 tbsp caster sugar
250 ml/9 fl oz milk
3 tbsp milk, for glazing
classic strawberry jam
(see page 120) and clotted
cream, to serve

method

1 Preheat the oven to 220°C/425°F/Gas Mark 7. Lightly flour a baking tray.

2 Sift the flour, salt and baking powder into a bowl. Rub in the butter until the mixture resembles breadcrumbs. Stir in the sugar. Make a well in the centre and pour in the milk. Stir in using a round-bladed knife and make a soft dough.

3 Turn the mixture onto a floured work surface and lightly flatten the dough until it is an even thickness, about 1 cm/½ inch. Don't be too heavy-handed – scones need a light touch.

4 Use a 6-cm/2½-inch pastry cutter to cut out the scones, then place them on the prepared baking tray. Glaze with a little milk and bake in the preheated oven for 10–12 minutes, until golden and well risen.

5 Leave to cool on a wire rack and serve freshly baked with strawberry jam and clotted cream.

strawberry shortcakes

ingredients

serves 6

225 g/8 oz self-raising flour,
    plus extra for dusting
½ tsp baking powder
100 g/3½ oz golden
    caster sugar
85 g/3 oz unsalted butter,
    plus extra for greasing
1 egg, beaten
2–3 tbsp milk, plus extra
    for brushing

filling

1 tsp vanilla extract
250 g/9 oz
    mascarpone cheese
3 tbsp icing sugar, plus extra
    for dusting
400 g/14 oz strawberries

method

1 Preheat the oven to 180°C/350°F/Gas Mark 4. Lightly grease a large baking tray.

2 Sift the flour, baking powder and sugar together into a bowl. Rub in the butter until the mixture resembles breadcrumbs. Beat the egg with 2 tablespoons of the milk. Stir into the dry ingredients with a fork to form a soft, but not sticky, dough, adding more milk if needed.

3 Turn out the dough onto a lightly floured surface and roll out to about 2 cm/¾ inch thick. Stamp out rounds, using a 7-cm/2¾-inch biscuit cutter. Lightly press the trimmings together and stamp out more rounds.

4 Place on the baking tray and brush the tops lightly with milk. Bake for 12–15 minutes, until firm and golden brown. Place on a wire rack to cool.

5 To make the filling, stir the vanilla extract into the cheese with 2 tablespoons of the sugar. Reserve a few whole strawberries for decoration, then hull and slice the rest. Sprinkle with the remaining sugar.

6 Split the shortcakes in half horizontally. Spoon half the cheese mixture onto the bases and top with the sliced strawberries. Spoon over the remaining cheese mixture and replace the tops. Dust the shortcakes with icing sugar and top with the reserved whole strawberries.

cinnamon swirls

ingredients
makes 12 swirls

225 g/8 oz strong white flour
½ tsp salt
10 g/¼ oz easy-blend dried yeast
2 tbsp butter, cut into small pieces,
    plus extra for greasing
1 egg, lightly beaten
125 ml/4 fl oz lukewarm milk
2 tbsp maple syrup, for glazing

filling

4 tbsp butter, softened
2 tsp ground cinnamon
50 g/1¾ oz soft light brown sugar
50 g/1¾ oz currants

method

1 Grease a baking sheet with a little butter.

2 Sift the flour and salt into a mixing bowl. Stir in the yeast. Rub in the butter with your fingertips until the mixture resembles breadcrumbs. Add the egg and milk and mix to form a dough.

3 Form the dough into a ball, place in a greased bowl, cover and leave to stand in a warm place for about 40 minutes, or until doubled in size.

4 Lightly knock back the dough for 1 minute, then roll out to a rectangle measuring 30 x 23 cm/12 x 9 inches.

5 To make the filling, cream together the butter, cinnamon and sugar until light and fluffy. Spread the filling evenly over the dough rectangle, leaving a 2.5-cm/1-inch border all around. Sprinkle the currants evenly over the top.

6 Roll up the dough from one of the long edges, and press down to seal. Cut the roll into 12 slices. Place them, cut-side down, on the baking sheet, cover and leave to stand for 30 minutes.

7 Meanwhile, preheat the oven to 190°C/375°F/Gas Mark 5. Bake the buns in the preheated oven for 20–30 minutes, or until well risen. Brush with the maple syrup and leave to cool slightly before serving.

apple streusel cake

ingredients

serves 8

450 g/1 lb cooking apples
175 g/6 oz self-raising flour
1 tsp ground cinnamon
pinch of salt
115 g/4 oz butter, plus extra for
    greasing
115 g/4 oz caster sugar
2 eggs
1–2 tbsp milk
icing sugar, for dusting

streusel topping

115 g/4 oz self-raising flour
85 g/3 oz butter
85 g/3 oz caster sugar

method

1 Preheat the oven to 180°C/350°F/Gas Mark 4, then grease a 23-cm/9-inch springform cake tin. To make the streusel topping, sift the flour into a bowl and rub in the butter until the mixture resembles coarse breadcrumbs. Stir in the sugar and reserve.

2 To make the cake, peel, core and thinly slice the apples. Sift the flour into a bowl with the cinnamon and salt. Place the butter and sugar in a separate bowl and beat together until light and fluffy. Gradually beat in the eggs, adding a little of the flour mixture with the last addition of egg. Gently fold in half the remaining flour mixture, then fold in the rest with the milk.

3 Spoon the mixture into the prepared tin and smooth the top. Cover with the sliced apples and sprinkle the streusel topping evenly over the top.

4 Bake in the preheated oven for 1 hour, or until browned and firm to the touch. Leave to cool in the tin before opening the sides. Dust the cake with icing sugar before serving.

victoria sponge cake

ingredients

serves 8–10

175 g/6 oz butter, at room
    temperature, plus
    extra for greasing
175 g/6 oz caster sugar
3 eggs, beaten
175 g/6 oz self-raising flour
pinch of salt
raspberry jam
double cream, whipped
1 tbsp icing sugar or caster sugar,
    for dusting

method

1 Preheat the oven to 180°C/350°F/Gas Mark 4.
Grease two 20-cm/8-inch sponge tins and line with
greaseproof paper or baking paper.

2 Cream the butter and sugar together in a mixing bowl
using a wooden spoon or a hand-held mixer until the
mixture is pale in colour and light and fluffy. Add the
eggs a little at a time, beating well after each addition.

3 Sift the flour and salt together and carefully add to the
mixture, folding in with a metal spoon or a spatula.
Divide the mixture between the tins and smooth over
with the spatula.

4 Place them on the same shelf in the centre of the
preheated oven and bake for 25–30 minutes until well
risen, golden brown and beginning to shrink from the
sides of the tins.

5 Remove from the oven and leave to stand for
1 minute. Loosen the cakes from around the edges of
the tins using a palette knife. Turn the cakes out onto a
clean tea towel, remove the paper and invert them
onto a wire rack. When completely cool, sandwich
together with the jam and cream and sprinkle with
icing sugar.

blueberry crumb cake

ingredients

serves 12

280 g/10 oz fresh blueberries
450 g/1 lb self-raising flour, plus
    extra for dusting
1¼ tsp salt
½ tsp mixed spice
280 g/10 oz butter, at room
    temperature, plus extra for
    greasing
350 g/12 oz caster sugar
½ tsp vanilla extract
½ tsp almond extract
2 large eggs
300–350 ml/10–12 fl oz
    soured cream

crumb topping

115 g/4 oz butter, diced
140 g/5 oz plain flour
2 tbsp soft light brown sugar
1 tbsp granulated sugar
85 g/3 oz almonds, chopped

method

1 To make the crumb topping, rub the butter into the flour until the mixture resembles coarse breadcrumbs. Stir in both types of sugar and the almonds, then leave to chill in the refrigerator.

2 Preheat the oven to 180°C/350°F/Gas Mark 4. Grease a 33 x 23-cm/13 x 9-inch rectangular cake tin and dust with flour. Dust the blueberries with 1 tablespoon of the flour and set aside. Sift the remaining flour into a bowl with the salt and mixed spice and set aside.

3 Place the butter in a large bowl and, using an electric mixer, beat until soft and creamy. Add the sugar, vanilla extract and almond extract and continue beating until the mixture is light and fluffy. Beat in the eggs one at a time, then beat in 300 ml/10 fl oz of the soured cream. Beat in the flour until the mixture is soft and falls easily from a spoon. Add the remaining soured cream, 1 tablespoon at a time.

4 Add the blueberries and any loose flour to the batter and quickly fold in. Pour the batter into the prepared tin and smooth the surface. Pinch the topping into large crumbs and scatter evenly over the batter.

5 Bake in the preheated oven for 45–55 minutes until it comes away from the side of the tin. Transfer the tin to a wire rack and leave to cool completely before slicing.

lemon drizzle cake

ingredients

serves 8

butter, for greasing
200 g/7 oz plain flour
2 tsp baking powder
200 g/7 oz caster sugar
4 eggs
150 ml/5 fl oz soured cream
grated rind of 1 large lemon
4 tbsp lemon juice
150 ml/5 fl oz sunflower oil

syrup

4 tbsp icing sugar
3 tbsp lemon juice

method

1 Preheat the oven to 180°C/350°F/Gas Mark 4. Lightly grease a 20-cm/8-inch loose-based round cake tin and line the base with baking paper.

2 Sift the flour and baking powder together into a mixing bowl and stir in the sugar.

3 In a separate bowl, whisk the eggs, soured cream, lemon rind, lemon juice and oil together.

4 Pour the egg mixture into the dry ingredients and mix well until evenly combined.

5 Pour the mixture into the prepared tin and bake in the preheated oven for 45–60 minutes, until risen and golden brown.

6 Meanwhile, to make the syrup, mix the icing sugar and lemon juice together in a small saucepan. Stir over a low heat until just beginning to bubble and turn syrupy.

7 As soon as the cake comes out of the oven, prick the surface with a fine skewer, then brush the syrup over the top. Leave the cake to cool completely in the tin before turning out and serving.

angel food cake

ingredients

serves 10

sunflower oil, for greasing
8 large egg whites
1 tsp cream of tartar
1 tsp almond extract
250 g/9 oz caster sugar
115 g/4 oz plain flour,
    plus extra for dusting

to serve

250 g/9 oz summer berries
1 tbsp lemon juice
2 tbsp icing sugar

method

1 Preheat the oven to 160°C/325°F/Gas Mark 3. Brush the inside of a 1.7-litre/3-pint ring tin with oil and dust lightly with flour.

2 Whisk the egg whites in a clean, grease-free bowl until they hold soft peaks. Add the cream of tartar and whisk again until the whites are stiff but not dry.

3 Whisk in the almond extract, then add the sugar, a tablespoon at a time, whisking hard between each addition. Sift in the flour and fold in lightly and evenly, using a large metal spoon.

4 Spoon the mixture into the prepared cake tin and tap on the work surface to remove any large air bubbles. Bake in the preheated oven for 40–45 minutes, or until golden brown and firm to the touch.

5 Run the tip of a small knife around the edges of the cake to loosen it from the tin. Leave to cool in the tin for 10 minutes, then turn out onto a wire rack to finish cooling.

6 To serve, place the berries, lemon juice and icing sugar in a saucepan and heat gently until the sugar has dissolved. Serve with the cake.

devil's food cake

ingredients

serves 8–10

140 g/5 oz plain chocolate, broken
   into pieces
100 ml/3½ fl oz milk
2 tbsp cocoa powder
140 g/5 oz unsalted butter, plus
   extra for greasing
140 g/5 oz light muscovado sugar
3 eggs, separated
4 tbsp soured cream or
   crème fraîche
200 g/7 oz plain flour
1 tsp bicarbonate of soda

frosting

140 g/5 oz plain chocolate, broken
   into pieces
40 g/1½ oz cocoa powder
4 tbsp soured cream or
   crème fraîche
1 tbsp golden syrup
40 g/1½ oz unsalted butter
4 tbsp water
200 g/7 oz icing sugar

method

1 Preheat the oven to 160°C/325°F/Gas Mark 3. Grease two 20-cm/8-inch sandwich tins and line the bases with non-stick baking paper.

2 Place the chocolate, milk and cocoa powder in a bowl over a saucepan of simmering water and heat gently, stirring, until melted. Remove from the heat.

3 In a large bowl beat the butter and muscovado sugar together until pale and fluffy. Beat in the egg yolks, the soured cream and the melted chocolate mixture. Sift in the flour and bicarbonate of soda, then fold in evenly. In a separate bowl, whisk the egg whites until stiff, then fold into the mixture lightly and evenly.

4 Divide the mixture between the cake tins, smooth level and bake in the preheated oven for 35–40 minutes, or until risen and firm to the touch. Cool in the tins for 10 minutes, then turn out onto a wire rack.

5 To make the frosting, put all the ingredients, apart from the icing sugar, into a saucepan and heat gently, until melted. Remove from the heat and sift in the sugar, stirring until smooth. Cool, stirring occasionally, until the mixture begins to thicken and hold its shape.

6 Split the cakes in half horizontally to make four layers. Sandwich them together with about a third of the frosting. Spread the remainder over the top and sides.

oat & potato bread

ingredients

makes 1 loaf

vegetable oil, for greasing
225 g/8 oz floury potatoes
500 g/1 lb 2 oz strong white flour,
    plus extra for dusting
1½ tsp salt
40 g/1½ oz butter, diced
1½ tsp easy-blend dried yeast
1½ tbsp soft dark brown sugar
3 tbsp rolled oats
2 tbsp skimmed milk powder
210 ml/7½ fl oz lukewarm water

topping

1 tbsp water
1 tbsp rolled oats

method

1 Grease a 900-g/2-lb loaf tin. Put the potatoes in a large saucepan, add water to cover and bring to the boil. Cook for 20–25 minutes, until tender. Drain, then mash until smooth. Leave to cool.

2 Sift the flour and salt together into a warmed bowl. Rub in the butter with your fingertips. Stir in the yeast, sugar, oats and milk powder. Mix in the mashed potato, then add the water and mix to a soft dough.

3 Turn out the dough onto a lightly floured work surface and knead for 5–10 minutes, or until smooth and elastic. Brush a bowl with oil and put the dough into it, cover with clingfilm and leave to rise in a warm place for 1 hour, or until doubled in size.

4 Turn out the dough again and knead lightly. Shape into a loaf and transfer to the prepared tin. Cover and leave to rise in a warm place for 30 minutes. Meanwhile, preheat the oven to 220°C/425°F/Gas Mark 7.

5 To make the topping, brush the surface of the loaf with the water and carefully sprinkle over the oats. Bake in the preheated oven for 25–30 minutes, or until it sounds hollow when tapped on the base. Transfer to a wire rack and leave to cool slightly. Serve warm.

cornbread

ingredients

makes 1 small loaf

vegetable oil, for greasing
175 g/6 oz plain flour
1 tsp salt
4 tsp baking powder
1 tsp caster sugar
280 g/10 oz quick-cook polenta
115 g/4 oz butter, softened
4 eggs
250 ml/9 fl oz milk
3 tbsp double cream

method

1 Preheat the oven to 200°C/400°F/Gas Mark 6. Brush a 20-cm/8-inch square cake tin with oil.

2 Sift the flour, salt and baking powder together into a bowl. Add the sugar and polenta and stir to mix. Add the butter and cut into the dry ingredients with a knife, then rub it in with your fingertips until the mixture resembles fine breadcrumbs.

3 Lightly beat the eggs in a bowl with the milk and cream, then stir into the polenta mixture until thoroughly combined.

4 Spoon the mixture into the prepared tin and smooth the surface. Bake in the preheated oven for 30–35 minutes, until a wooden cocktail stick inserted into the centre of the loaf comes out clean. Remove the tin from the oven and leave to cool for 5–10 minutes, then cut into squares and serve warm.

variation

To add extra flavour and colour, deseed and skin one large red pepper. Dice finely and fold into the mixture. Or add one red chilli, deseeded and finely chopped.

index